Cynthia "Sissy" Hogue and I have been friends for over forty years. My husband was her best friend until I came along. Around sixteen years ago, Sissy told me she was going to write a book, to this I replied OK, knowing in my heart that she would and being led by God she did. February of 2020, during a very sad time in our lives, she told me it was finished. This book "Permission", is an easy, comforting and enjoyable read that will inspire and give pause for thought. It spoke to my spirit as I believe it can speak to yours. This was a true labor of love and it was done for you. Get comfy and ENJOY!

—JoAnne Perry
PS:Sissy, this is a piece of the life I sing about in my song.

Permission is extraordinary read, new and stimulating in an interesting and unusual way. Written in conversation style, the book will captivate any reader. Something Cynthia read years ago really rings true in this work: just write it like you would speak or talk it. That's what you will get in this work—good fresh, down to earth conversation from a woman who has God's permission to be herself. This book is on –point and easy to digest. At the same time, you will be both encouraged and challenged by what is said. Permission to be who God called and ordained you to be is the touchstone of this writing. It can be a life changer if you grab hold of its content. Be blessed as you read.

—Pastor's jerry and Wilma Johnson
Beacon of Light International Ministries
Kansas City, Missouri

"Permission" helps us to understand that the search for place and purpose in this world is a spiritual journey and that giving yourself permission to be who you are intended to be is an internal process that often conflicts with the external world. This book will guide you toward your growth and your truth. It instructs you to trust yourself in relation to God, his word and the process. It frees you from the restraint of judgment and self-doubt, increasing your spirituality with freedom from religion. We are called to greatness in our relationship with God. He will translate and speak to you what is for you. "Permission" expresses the truth that God's love is customized for each of us because each journey is different. His relenting grace and mercy is a universal process afforded to all who are willing to ask. Be Well, Be Blessed and be You in Jesus name.

—Ila Debose, LCSW, UA Fort Smith

Permission is a book that we all can identify with. Some of the life experiences that Minister Hogue shared in the book, we may have experienced ourselves. And if we are in that process right now prayerfully "Permission" will help you get the breakthrough you need to turn your life around.

Minister Hogue has given the reader valuable and practical information along with Christian principles that we can use to make our Christian journey most effective.

I would implore you to get a journal, a highlighter and your favorite drink and allow permission to change your life. As you read Permission and journal, let this book saturate your thought, dreams and visions. Let go and Let God.

Love, Peace and Happiness
—Rev. Gary O Perry

Thanks you Cynthia for this gift. This book is very easy to read and most of all very understandable. The life experiences were heart-felt and at times would bring you in on the emotional state of the writer. One of the best parts is the fact that there are scriptures to support the conversation that is going on. I was moved to tears and overwhelming joy at the same time by the question "where is she". This book is filled with power, clarity, and conviction that causes the one who reads it wanting more.

—Pastor Wesley Hooks

PERMISSION

It's in You

CYNTHIA HOGUE

Copyright © 2021 Cynthia Hogue.

All rights reserved. No part of this book may be used or reproduced by any means, graphic, electronic, or mechanical, including photocopying, recording, taping or by any information storage retrieval system without the written permission of the author except in the case of brief quotations embodied in critical articles and reviews.

This book is a work of non-fiction. Unless otherwise noted, the author and the publisher make no explicit guarantees as to the accuracy of the information contained in this book and in some cases, names of people and places have been altered to protect their privacy.

WestBow Press books may be ordered through booksellers or by contacting:

WestBow Press
A Division of Thomas Nelson & Zondervan
1663 Liberty Drive
Bloomington, IN 47403
www.westbowpress.com
844-714-3454

Because of the dynamic nature of the Internet, any web addresses or links contained in this book may have changed since publication and may no longer be valid. The views expressed in this work are solely those of the author and do not necessarily reflect the views of the publisher, and the publisher hereby disclaims any responsibility for them.

Any people depicted in stock imagery provided by Getty Images are models, and such images are being used for illustrative purposes only. Certain stock imagery © Getty Images.

Cover Design by Jemel Parker - Pivotal Mix LLC

ISBN: 978-1-6642-3003-3 (sc)
ISBN: 978-1-6642-3004-0 (hc)
ISBN: 978-1-6642-3002-6 (e)

Library of Congress Control Number: 2021906706

Print information available on the last page.

WestBow Press rev. date: 10/1/2021

Unless otherwise indicated, all Scripture taken from the King James Version of the Bible.

Scripture quotations marked (NIV) are taken from the Holy Bible, New International Version®, NIV®. Copyright © 1973, 1978, 1984, 2011 by Biblica, Inc.® Used by permission of Zondervan. All rights reserved worldwide. www.zondervan.com The "NIV" and "New International Version" are trademarks registered in the United States Patent and Trademark Office by Biblica, Inc.®

Scripture quotations marked (CEV) are from the Contemporary English Version Copyright © 1991, 1992, 1995 by American Bible Society, Used by Permission.

Scripture quotations marked (NLT) are taken from the Holy Bible, New Living Translation, copyright ©1996, 2004, 2015 by Tyndale House Foundation. Used by permission of Tyndale House Publishers, a Division of Tyndale House Ministries, Carol Stream, Illinois 60188. All rights reserved.

Scripture marked (Weymouth) taken from the Weymouth New Testament.

Scripture quotations marked (NASB) taken from the New American Standard Bible® (NASB), Copyright © 1960, 1962, 1963, 1968, 1971, 1972, 1973, 1975, 1977, 1995 by The Lockman Foundation Used by permission. www.Lockman.org

Scripture quotations marked (GNT) are from the Good News Translation in Today's English Version- Second Edition Copyright © 1992 by American Bible Society. Used by Permission.

Scripture quotations marked MSG are taken from THE MESSAGE, copyright © 1993, 2002, 2018 by Eugene H. Peterson. Used by permission of NavPress. All rights reserved. Represented by Tyndale House Publishers, a Division of Tyndale House Ministries.

To Michelle, Thell Jr., Summer, and Jemel

You are my heroes, my inspiration and the reason I leave this legacy as a reminder of who you are created to be. One day, your dad and I will not be here, and you will face something that you believe you can't overcome—but you can and you will because of who you are.

Your love, support, laughter, encouragement, belief, questions, conversations, and dedication to your parents are without a doubt my stabling force, my life work, and my true joy. You hold my heart. I thank the Lord that He chose me for you and you for me.

To Jarret, Stacey, and Stephnie

It is an honor to be your bonus mom.

To my husband, Glen, for all you have brought to me—the good, the bad, and the ugly

The tests grounded me, molded me, and laid me on the altar. The love pulled me out of me, sustained me, and helped me to see the trees from the forest (yes, I know the idiom is reversed). Love you infinity.

CONTENTS

Lessons Learned xi
Preface xiii
Acknowledgments xix
Introduction xxiii

Chapter 1   The Book 1
Chapter 2   Mirror, Mirror 9
Chapter 3   Beware the Power of Religion 15
Chapter 4   Walk with Me 25
Chapter 5   Privilege 31
Chapter 6   You Can Change 37
Chapter 7   Warfare 45
Chapter 8   The End Is Just the Beginning 55

Afterword 63

LESSONS LEARNED

As I try to get this book published, I am learning there are many legalities, processes and steps to audit before one ever gets to the publishing stage. Many of the issues that arise are understandable, but to the author we just want our words to show up in print just as we initially wrote them, after all it's our book. I was in the last stages before final review and design and there is one more issue to resolve. That issue was the very reason this book came to be. This entire project is based on the knowledge of knowing and being certain that you can converse with God and expect to receive an answer.

As you read this book, please know and believe that God does hear you and that He will respond to you in ways you cannot imagine. Had I not invested so much time, energy, and money into this manuscript, I would have terminated the project. *But* my mission and my goal are to see all of us being continually transformed by the Word of God, yet even in this process, there is reason for the trial. Furthermore, to ensure that you are not confused and that the message and integrity of this manuscript is not compromised, I had to overcome my frustration and make the necessary changes to comply with the standards the editing team had set forth.

I was told by the editing team that I could not directly quote what God would say to me because we don't know what God says unless it's in the Bible. Ironically, having a conversation with God is the very crux of this work. I do realize these are publishing guidelines but generally such an attitude is one of the reasons why people fail to believe and embrace God. As you read your Bible and the Word begins to speak to you from that spirit place, and as we are on this journey, searching and asking questions, putting our faith into action, and, finally, as spirits housed in these human bodies, our ability to call upon God and know that He is listening and will respond becomes our most desperate plea.

In this manuscript, I attempt to share with you some of the most important times that God spoke to me. I simply state that my spirit spoke to me, or I use the term *spiritual significance* as the header for the paragraph, just to give clarification and credibility as to how and from whom the communication came to me. And those communications were consistent with the Word of God.

I have made many edits, all the while remembering how the people of Christ will win in the last days: "And they overcame him by the blood of the lamb, and by the word of their testimony: and they loved not their lives unto the death" (Revelation 12:11). This too is how you and I will win in our daily battles to overcome the things of the world and remain aligned and true to His Word.

We are spirit beings, and it is that very spirit in us that is regenerated and allows us to hear the Word of God. Once we get back to self and identify and agree with the God in us, those conversations become clear.

This manuscript has been a labor of love. And going through this process has tested my patience and perseverance and has allowed me to see a portion of God's purpose for my life. As I labor to cross the last *t* and dot the last *i,* I will ask and pray and pray and ask until the final edit has been completed and this manuscript has met the standard of the publishing company and the purpose of the vision given to me.

PREFACE

Webster's definition of *permission* is "the act of permitting, formal consent: authorization."

Other definitions are as follows:

> Strongs Concordance 2011: full allowance

> *Strong's Concordance with Hebrew and Greek Lexicon/ Condensed Brown-Driver-Briggs Hebrew Lexicon*: H7990: having mastery, having authority, it is authorized

> Online Etymology Dictionary: Permit: Latin, *Per* (forward)-*Mittere* (through), let pass, let go, let loose

There was not any one issue that prompted the birth of this book. But a myriad of life issues that caused me to seek answers that would resolve or give me peace in those situations. Family issues, work issues and issues with who I was and how I was handling any given situation. My hope and prayer as you begin to read this book is that you feel a sense of *this is just what I needed at this particular time*. I pray that you are able to see yourself in these pages. Get something to drink, put on your pj's, turn on some good worship music, or settle down in blessed quietness, if you prefer. Read and ponder, read and think, read and meditate, read and scribble, and read and say, "Hmmm." You have permission to do whatever you want to do. This is your time.

Our struggles may not be the same, but I believe that we as a collective group of people, share some of the same issues, feelings, and uncertainties, the same fears and loneliness. I believe that as the issues of life happen to use in the form of sickness, divorce, birth, death, marriage, job loss, financial loss and all the issues that make up what we call life struggles, that we ask the same questions during these difficult times. I have been in all those places and I just believe that some of you are just as lost as I was as I wandered in and out of that season of uncertainty—that season of not knowing who I was, what I was to do, or how I was to do it. I was afraid and empty.

I did one thing that changed the course and put me on the path to purpose. I went to church. I consistently went to church. I became involved. And then the amazing happened. God favored me. Deep in my spirit, I heard my name being called. My heart, my mind, and my soul were open to receive. More importantly, my spirit answered and the only thing I knew to do was to return to the house of the Lord.

I realize that it is not always about attending church but attending regular worship is a great starting point. To be in the fellowship of likeminded individuals gives us strength, both emotionally and spiritually. I personally know people who are very negative when it comes to attending worship. Often times we think, *I don't need to go to church. I'm just as good as anyone else without church,* and you are. But going to the church house is where we find that there are hurting people just like you and me who need some relief. I cannot tell you what to do. I can only suggest. But I can tell you this: the Bible says,

> Some people have given up the habit of meeting for worship, but we must not do that. We should keep on encouraging each other, especially since you know that the day of the Lord's coming is getting closer. (Hebrews 10:25 Contemporary English Version)

We learn in the sanctuary. You must always do what you think is best for you, but consider the results: we need the church, the gathering of the saints. We need the teaching, the fellowship, and the accountability of the preached Word. There is no greater place to learn of God than in His house, in His presence. Just try it, you have everything to gain.

John Gill's exposition of the Bible on Psalm 73:17 expresses it best:

> Until I went into the sanctuary of God. The tabernacle or house of God, where the Word of God was read and explained, prayer was made, and sacrifices offered up, and where fellowship was had with the saints, and communion with God himself; which for one hour or moment is preferable to all the prosperity of the wicked, during their whole life. This shows that though the psalmist was beset with the temptation, yet not overcome; it did not so far prevail as to cause him to neglect public worship, and relinquish the house of God, and the ordinances of it; and it is right, under temptations, doubts, and difficulties, to attend the public ministrations, which is the way and means to have relief under temptations, to have doubts resolved, and difficulties removed: some by "the sanctuary of God" understand the Scriptures, which are holy and of God, and are profitable for instruction, and are to be consulted and entered into by a serious reading of and deep meditation on them; whereby may be known the happiness that is prepared for the saints in the other world, and the misery of the wicked, and hereby judgment may be made of the present case and condition of each: others interpret it of the world of spirits, which may be entered into by contemplation; when it may be observed that the spirits of just men upon their dissolution possess unspeakable joys and glories, and the souls of the wicked are in inconceivable torments: then understood I their end; both of the godly and of the wicked; that the end of the righteous is peace, rest, salvation, and eternal life, and the end of the wicked is ruin, destruction, and death.

I knew I could hear God. I knew that I was in communication with the one who could answer all my questions and that my spirit was receiving. Thus, the journey began.

Some years ago, we had a team-building event. It was my turn to plan the exercise. I asked everyone to bring a gift, a token—something they treasured and did not expect to get it back. As we gathered, the gifts were laid out on a table and numbered. Each participant was asked to choose a gift. As the gifts were revealed the person who brought that particular gift was asked to share why the gift was so personal to them. In doing so we learned things we did not know about that person. We saw their heart in some of the responses. Some were very personal. My giveaway was my book *Conversations with God*. It was my book—until I became acquainted with the Bible. I had written on its pages, turned down page corners, and highlighted certain passages. It had been folded, highlighted, and creased. I had referred to the pages many times. I didn't want to give it up, but I had set the rules. I looked for other treasures that might fit the criteria I had set forth, but it was the book, and I knew instinctively that whoever got this book needed it as much as I had when I'd wandered upon it. The book has a story that was personal to me.

I was attending a Sunday school class and one of the attendees asked a question. I can't remember the content of the question but I do remember the answer. (Honestly, the class was boring, and the teacher was not excited about the lesson, but the answer caught my attention.) At this time, I was looking for God, looking for answers, and nothing was coming in.

The teacher answered, "God does not really speak to man." There was no point of reference, just those words. Those seven words caused me to sit up and take notice.

I wanted to raise my hand, but I didn't think I knew enough to ask a question. So I thought, *If God doesn't speak to us in some manner, then how will I know what to do? If He doesn't speak to us, how do we repent, ask forgiveness, and ultimately know that we have been forgiven?* I wanted and needed so badly to hear from Him.

I left that class very confused. I felt worse than I had felt when I entered the class, so much so that I did not stay for the morning service.

Then I came across a book on the reduced-price book table at the bookstore—*Conversations with God* by Neale Donald Walsch. The title alone caught my eye, and my spirit leaped because I was desperate for a conversation with God. This title gave me hope. I didn't understand that I had been conversing back and forth with Him all along, and my spirit had been receiving the answers to my questions. I was not astute enough to know and understand that I was hearing within my spirit, and I didn't understand the full implication of what was happening—at least not at that time.

I bought the book, but I put it on a shelf at home and did not read it right away. When I did, it changed my life and opened my mind to the *more* of God. I knew I was on to something. I referred to it many times, and eventually, I shared it with someone else. (Keep reading; you will see.) But guess what? Sometime later, I was doing my usual bookstore browsing, and there, on the sale table, was *The Complete Conversations with God: Books I, II and III*. I felt like I had found a treasure—and the journey began. I was on my way.

The answer came before I knew the question. I was at a fork in the road, but I knew I was going where God was.

ACKNOWLEDGMENTS

Pastor Jerry and Pastor Wilma: thank you for fueling my fire. I don't think I could have completed this work without the level of learning and discipline that you both have mentored.

Rev. Kimble: thank you for putting away tradition and throwing all your weight around a female minister in the Baptist Church. I am sure you took a lot of righteous condemnation for that move.

Kimberly Parker: thank you for exhibiting kindness, love, and belief in me when I believed that those qualities could not be restored.

Rev. Gary O and Sister Karen Perry: thank you for waiting on me to get to the place I was destined to be.

Kathy Coleman: you came to me when I asked, not knowing who I was or what you would be getting into after agreeing to be a speaker at our prayer breakfast. You are an example that shows that we never know who will be the one to help us or to have a word for us. You spoke about "perfectness" and how you thought you had to have the perfect family, the perfect husband and children, to be validated. Then you woke up and realized it was about you and your mission—the mission God gave you.

There was a particular day I was at home cleaning going back and forth down the stairs with an arms full of laundry and cleaning supplies. As I was descending the stairs about midway down, I stopped. My spirit spoke, *Release him and give him back to me.* I knew exactly what that meant. I had to let go of attempting to fix everything. Kathy's message on that day was a direct result of this surrender.

There is freedom in surrender. I thought everything had to be perfect for me to carry out God's work. It did not. I only had to be obedient to His will.

Pastor Tina Releford: thank you for being a trailblazer and for showing honor when it was not always shown to you.

Belva Jean: thank you for hearing the sure Word and for your steadfastness to me.

Joanne Perry: once in a lifetime we are gifted with a true friend—one who loves unconditionally and without reservation or regard to what's been done or to what will be done; one who looks at you, sees you, and then prays for the things you cannot see and holds those things in her heart until they are ready to be released; one who keeps you and your family on her lips in prayer and calls out your name to God in heaven. I pray I have loved you as honorably as you have loved us.

To my village

I did not have a true appreciation of (and never gave much thought to) the village until my cousin died in 2017. At the funeral, I saw the village come together to say goodbye, and all I could think was, *It takes a village*. This statement is so much more than those words; its blood, sweat, and tears. It's a group of people working together towards a common goal. The village assumes responsibility for its own and in the village, everyone shares and helps each other. No one is alone or left out, unless one chooses to be. The village is a place of refuge, safety, and shelter and often pain. Sadly, it is the very pain of the village that drove us away. Funny—once we reconcile the pain in some way, we feel a longing to return to the village. Some leave and never return. I know some of those people, and I have come to realize that there is a longing in them that never subsides. Those who remain are the ones who keep the fires burning—reminiscent of the Motel 6 slogan, "We'll leave the lights on for you."

The village is a special place that holds a certain power and intimacy with people who have shared in your life. It knows your family, your history, and your secrets. It knows who and where I came from and to whom I belong. The village protects the teachings and traditions of the elders and teaches us about holding on and letting go.

My village, you have surrounded me with pride and with power. You have provided me with the knowledge that the village is always willing and ready to come to my rescue, whether good or not so good. The village is our safe place; the place we find solace; the place we find our joy again. We know how the village operates because we were once held in its clutches until we felt we needed to break free. But we always, in some way, come back, and you always accept us with open arms. The village fights for you to win. My prayer is that the village will not die off without someone to honor those traditions and carry on its legacy, to tell its stories, to secure its secrets, to mend our hearts, and to advise our comings and goings. My village lives in me and has helped to mold me and to shape the character within me. As my grandmother would say, "it's in you". To my village, as long as you are there, I will tell your stories and keep you alive.

INTRODUCTION

Thank you for picking up this book. In my mind, I have seen this book come to fruition.

It started with a scripture and then a question. Quo vadis, or where are you going?

Permission

> For God so loved the world, that he gave his only begotten Son, that whosoever believeth in him should not perish, but have everlasting life.
> —John 3:16

Along the way to finding the lost person inside of me, along the way to purpose, I ran into tribulation, distress and persecution. Some of my on doing, some at the hand of others. But along the way something happened. A new pastor was called to our congregation, he challenged and changed all of what I thought I knew and all I thought I was to Christ. He explained that this gospel thing was all about me. That I mattered to God.

We were in a Wednesday night Bible class. The teacher was speaking on how to wait on God and that we are to keep our flesh under "subjection" Somehow, we ended up at John 3:16. Almost everyone can quote this scripture verbatim or some parts of it. It's probably the first scripture we memorized as children, yet we only touch the surface of what it means. We only touch the surface of its real substance. It's full of meat, in the sense that someone died so we could live—and not just live now but eternally.

Songs have tried to express the meaning, but until you actually see yourself, in all your dirt and filth and sin, you cannot know the debt that was paid for you and me. Until you can see yourself in this state of being, you cannot imagine, not in any way, what that love expressed. He came back for us.

From this scripture, we know that God loved the entire world, and because of His love for humankind, He sacrificed His only Son, His only child. If you and I and the world would just acknowledge that His Son was and is His only begotten, if we would confess our sins and repent, when we close our eyes for the last time and the breath leaves our bodies, that our spirit will go to Him and have an assurance of immortality. It is that immortality, that eternal existence that was lost, that He came back to reconcile.

The pastor said, "Take it seriously, and make it personal because this scripture is for you as an individual."

At that moment, I knew I was at the right place. He knew more than I did. He challenged me and pushed me to know more and to be able to express it. He made me move from that mountain of not knowing to discovering what was on the other side of the mountain. He said, "Once you begin to take this scripture personally, your life will change in ways that you cannot imagine." It's a learning scripture and one that is—I repeat—full of meat. This scripture singles you out, calls you out, and makes you aware that everything God planned before the foundation of the world was with *you* and me in mind. We are in His heart. There is no motive, except love. "For God so loved"—*so loved* is the deepest expression of love.

Love yourself—the good, the bad, and the ugly. Love your life. It is all happening for your good, to bring you to an expected end. Each day, speak life to yourself. Live in the "permissions" given to you by our Lord.

I will be excited to hear from you and to share in your struggles and successes. Prepare for more. Because of John 3:16, I am here.

However, as it is written: "What no eye has seen, what no ear has heard, and what no human mind has conceived"—the things God has prepared for those who love him. (1 Corinthians 2:9 NIV)

1

THE BOOK

When I discovered your words, I devoured them. They are my joy and my heart's delight, for I bear your name, O LORD God of Heaven's Armies.

—Jeremiah 15:16 (NLT)

I love books—the size, the color, the shapes, the artwork, the feel. Ah, the last page—I can always tell a good book by the last page. That's my formula. For me this is the part of the book that tells the story. This is the part of the book that tells me there is meat inside the pages for me to devour.

The last page tells the story just as the end of our lives tells the story of who we were, what we did, and how we got there. The end is the legacy we leave. As in the song my mama sings, the end tells others how we got over ("How I Got Over" by Mahalia Jackson). The story of "you".

My dream is to one day have a room so big that I can fill it with books and call it a library, with shelves so high that I would need a library ladder to pull a book for the day. And in the middle of the room, a big, fat, chamois-colored leather sofa. Ah, to dream.

As for the book, I wanted to pen something that would be easy on the eyes and on the mind. So many people, myself included, are simply looking for an easy read—simple answers to hard questions. So many books are bogged down by intellect and theology. This is not one of those books. So if you are searching, and you are tired and frustrated in body and mind, and you want—to coin a phrase—"just the facts, man," then this is that book. It's not that your mind is incapable of absorbing a theological treatise or that you're not intellectual enough to dissect the words and content. It's more that your mind is simply tired.

This book has gone through many titles, from *For My Girls*, to *All about You*, and then—here comes a word—*Permission*. My original intent was to write this to share my thoughts and the content with my girls only—just simple words of wisdom, life's challenges, how to operate and navigate this life, how to prepare and rise to any occasion, and, ultimately, how to live this life in preparation for the next life and how to be *you* in all situations.

As the apostle Paul said, "I have become all things to all people so that by all possible means I might save some" (1 Corinthians 9:22 NIV). In other words, as believers, one of our chief responsibilities is to win souls to Christ. We are to be successful examples and to be all things to all people so that we are able to reach people at whatever point in life they find themselves. How do we equip ourselves to respond to what I call those sudden moments? Those events that in an instant "Suddenly" can alter our lives in unexpected ways. *Suddenly, by Merriam-Webster's on line dictionary* is defined as quickly and unexpectedly, unforeseen, unanticipated, or abrupt.

Suddenly causes us to be as agitated, trouble, vexed. All these emotions happen in a very short span of time.

Suddenly, can change everything. Things will happen. Life will happen. What do we do? How do we respond? How do we manage—suddenly? It is those sudden moments that really mold and test us. The sudden moments pull the realness out of you and redirect you. *Suddenly* will require something of you and take something from you. If you are not prepared, sudden moments will leave you without and holding an empty bag. During sudden moments, we should be prepared to have an attitude, as Peter explains: "Beloved think it not strange concerning the fiery trial which is to try you, as though some strange thing happened unto you" (1 Peter 4:12).

As the words began to flow, I became acutely aware that the words were not just for my girls but for everyone's girls and boys and men and women everywhere. I have learned—possibly you have as well—that there is no handbook for parenting. As far as parenting lessons go, I have found three methodologies: we either do what our parents did, we do as we see others do, or we do what our instincts tell us to do. Parenting is the most challenging and rewarding job that a woman or a man will ever have. It seems that parents are constantly teetering between two places—holding on or letting go. There is rarely a consistent balance.

As a parent, watching my children become adults, I have realized their need for parenting as adults is far greater than when they were children. Our children's adult years will show you what type of parent you were. I have four children; they are the same but individually different. At their core—their values, morals, and intent—they are the same. Each of them has their own purpose and their own path to get there. They let us know when life is working and when life is not treating them so well. The key is that they let us know. We must always attempt to keep the lines of communication open. Scripture tells us that Lo, children are heritage from the Lord: and the fruit of the womb is his reward. (Psalm 127:3). God has entrusted you and I to care for his possession

One of the major tests of parenthood is that although we parents have the responsibility for our children, they will be influenced by many other people during the course of their lifetimes. Our responsibility is to set the foundation for them and to ensure that the foundation is as solid as we can reinforce it, so that when something comes along (and it will) that attempts to crack the foundation, our children will know what to do and how to rebuild.

It's the same solid foundation that our Lord has intended it to be for us, His children. As much as that pains us as parents, it's very true. We must be the best example we can be so that our children will be able to discern how they should move forward. Yes, we often fail, but thanks be to God for the grace to fall. I believe that only our cultural and ethnic differences bring about earthly separations. In His eyes, we are all the *same*. He is no respecter of persons. Our children, especially, need to realize this concept; otherwise, they will grow up with a sense of entitlement.

As my children reached adulthood, their life questions seemed to grow as well. Some things, I didn't want to know or deal with—you know, those TMI (too much information) questions. Looking back, I am thankful that I was able to speak to the issue or problem at hand, and I was thankful they trusted me enough to bring those issues to me. I wanted them to have something to refer back to, something to rely on.

And I want the same for you. We all need to know how to survive, how to climb out of the pit in which we may find ourselves. How do we make it? As I think back, I'm sure my children thought I was having some type of internal crisis when I enrolled in Ministry school, as well as when my call to preach came. I can only imagine the conversations they must have had among themselves.

This brings me to Job. The Bible states that Job had a regular custom—after his children had been together, feasting, he would pray for them to purify them.

> His sons used to hold feasts in their homes on their birthdays, and they would invite their three sisters to eat and drink with them. When a period of feasting had run its course, Job would make arrangements for them to be purified. Early in the morning he would sacrifice a burnt offering for each of them, thinking, "Perhaps my children have sinned and cursed God in their hearts." This was Job's regular custom. (Job 1:1–5 NIV)

Sages have been writing in some form since the beginning of time, recording lives, events, hopes, dreams, plans, failures, tragedies, and successes. Each of us has a story. Our stories are our testimonies to inspire, encourage, and support those who are on the same journey—a journey of self-discovery. Our stories are words to help another gain strength and are a testament to our having survived the storm. Our stories show that trouble doesn't last always; that joy truly does come in the morning; that weeping only endures for a night. And that with right teaching and support, you will survive. It's not easy, but it's possible with God. The Bible says so: "I can do all things through Christ which strengthened me" (Philippians 4:13).

I kept hearing in my spirit, *The book is your story, your key.* My mind was constantly throwing thoughts at me. And those thoughts were coming so fast that I had difficulty remembering them. I would have scraps of paper everywhere, entire tablets, and notes on any piece of paper I could and fill them with those thoughts, revelations, dreams, and prophetic utterances. Each time a thought or revelation came, I'd write it down. I didn't know what they were for or what I was going to do with them, but as time passed, God's word began to reveal things to me. This book is the result of those discourses.

I had difficulty compiling them into some kind of order. Then I heard, "Maybe that's the problem. You are trying to make an orderly book out of a disorderly, unorganized life." That made sense to me. Some years ago, I read an article that described how to begin writing. The author explained, "Just write it like you would speak it or talk it." That also made sense to me.

I heard in my spirit, "You get in the way of yourself. You focus on what you cannot control, things you cannot do anything about. And because of that, you can't effectively find a starting place. You need a plan that works for you. You are falling behind, and the world doesn't stop and will not stop to wait on you. You've had plenty of opportunity to start. Remember the word *opportunity* and its definition: a set of circumstances that have come together that makes it possible to do something or an amount of time or a situation in which something can be done. Grace is your opportunity. You always will have grace, but opportunity is fleeting. It comes to us in stages, and the opportunity presented is expressly for that stage of life. It cannot be duplicated for another stage. When opportunity shows its face to you again, you may not see or know that this is it; this is the time. Be ready. You possess all the necessary tools."

My journey became clearer when I made the decision to attend the Beacon of Light School of Ministry. Several people I knew were attending and encouraged me to attend with them. The leap I took to become a student of their school opened a new world for me. At first, I was hesitant to apply. I worried about what people would say. That brings me the first lesson: what people think of you will kill you. It will kill your hopes and dreams. My sister Kim says, "You can't share your dreams with everyone." That reminds me of all the things I wanted to do. Things I knew I could do that would make a difference but for some reason could not find a starting point.

Once I made the decision to attend I began the application process. To be accepted as a student one of the requirements was a letter of recommendation from my current pastor and an essay on why I wanted to attend the school of ministry.

I was a member of a Baptist Church. Baptist leaders are not too keen on their members exploring or wanting to be a part of anything that is not Baptist-affiliated. The basic tenants of who Christ is seemed to be only identifiable in the word Baptist. Therefore because Baptist is Baptist there was no common ground or any reason for the Pastor to approve or give a recommendation to attend any other denominational study. Additionally the curriculum at the school of ministry was taught by the senior Pastor of the church who just happened to be female. Few Baptist leaders believe or accept female minister's and certainly not behind the pulpit. As our world constantly changes women have stepped to the forefront of every challenge, every need, not so much out of want but out of need. God will use whoever He chooses—woman or man—to deliver His message of salvation to the masses.

I explained to the school board why I did not get the required recommendation and was given an exception to enter the program.

PERMISSION

We met twice a week. Pastor Jerry and Pastor Wilma Johnson who were our instructors opened the scriptures in a way that put us right smack in the center of the narrative. The visual representation of the word that was presented in each class was life altering. I loved the Word and the revelation and the knowledge those classes brought to my world.

Pastor Jerry and Pastor Wilma are my heroes of the faith. There are few who can talk the talk and walk the walk as they so faithfully do. Together they are a formidable team. And because of their dedication to the word and to seeing people grow and become, I gained the knowledge and the power to step into what I have been called to do.

My prayer is that this little book will guide you, comfort you, and help you along the way to simplicity and peace.

I present it to you with much love and hope, to help you over and through the rough patches. This book's purpose is to give you peace in a hectic world. Enjoy it, use it, and reference it. Most importantly, use it as a tool for your spiritual well-being.

MIRROR, MIRROR

> For the present we see things as if in a mirror, and are puzzled; but then we shall see them face to face. For the present the knowledge I gain is imperfect; but then I shall know fully, even as I am fully known.
>
> —1 Corinthians 13:12 (Weymouth New Testament)

Mirror, mirror on the wall, who's the fairest of them all?

Are those just words of a fairy tale? Oftentimes we are labeled by two distinct definitions and these definitions are also the standards by which we have been taught to define ourselves—the same two standards by which the world will define us:

1. The world's definition of you; how the world sees you; what the world says you can and cannot do
2. God's biblical definition of you and how the Word sees you; what God's Word says you can be; and what God's revelations

say you can do; all based on what God has deposited in you and if you are ready to harvest the deposit

In real-life scenarios, there is a third definition of *you*: how you see yourself. This is the one that will make or break you.

Do you know enough about yourself to speak to the *you* in *you*? Your power lies in what you speak to yourself. In perfect truth, there is no defense. Your spirit knows the truth. It lies there, unspoken. You must have the courage to be *you* because you cannot be an imitator of another human. You are to be an imitator of the one called Christ.

The world wants to keep us in a pretty decorated box that often is only opened when the world says the time is appropriate. That's very hard to do when the Word is speaking to us, calling us. We succeed or fail by the box in which we allow ourselves to be contained. It takes time to figure that out, and when we do figure it out, we wonder how we allowed *that* to contain us. The best of us can easily be led astray.

It doesn't matter what our title, financial situation, age, gender, race, or ethnicity is. We fall. We mess up. We make mistakes. But our falling—thanks be to God and the chances He has given us—can propel us back into right standing. We must remember that no matter how well put together we think we are, we were, at one time, aliens and strangers to God. Our falling is the very reason God wrapped Himself in flesh and came to us as Jesus Christ to fulfill a mission that belonged only to Him. He alone has the answers to our past, present, and future—the plan to reconcile us back to Him.

Today, you may look in the mirror, and the reflection staring back at you is someone you don't recognize. Today, everything is wrong. Today, you can't find the calm place. Today, the restlessness is overpowering. Today, you realize that today is the day. You speak to the *you* in the mirror, but that person is no longer there. She/he does not respond to your calls. Did you lose her/him, or did she/he lose you? How did she/he slip away without your noticing that she/

he was no longer there? I have a friend who says, "If you put up with a thing long enough, you become accustomed to it."

Years have come and gone, yet there remains a restlessness about you. There's a place in you, in your inner being, in your core that you can't calm. You can't identify it or put a name to it. It's just there—a forgotten place, a place that needs your attention but has been buried and neglected for so long because of the cares of life. It is now rising. It wants to breathe. It wants to live again. It has something to say and something to do. It has risen to a full crescendo and wants to claim its rightful place. It's *you*.

You want your life to have intent, purpose, and substance. You want your life to have life. Presently, it's just a series of repetitious actions—some necessary, some not—actions with little focus or meaning. You have become accustomed to routine, to things being this way because that's how they've always been. There's a silent scream, that only you can hear. Your light has dimmed—it's still there but dimmer. *Enough!*

"How did I get here? What happened to me?" you ask the mirror, as if the mirror will give you the answers you seek—the who, what, when, where, and why of life. "Who am I? What has happened? When did it happen? Where did it happen? Why did it happen?"

Who am I? You are who you have allowed yourself to be.

> A person may think their own ways are right, but the LORD weighs the heart. (Proverbs 21:2 NIV)

> There is a way that appears to be right, but in the end it leads to death. (Proverbs 16:25 NIV)

What do I do? Decide today that you will live with intent and purpose.

> In him we were also chosen, having been predestined according to the plan of him who works out everything in conformity with the purpose of his will. (Ephesians 1:11 NIV)

When do I start? Have I not commanded you?

> Be strong and courageous. Do not be afraid; do not be discouraged, for the LORD your God will be with you wherever you go. (Joshua 1:9 NIV)

Where do I go from here? Start where you are, do all you can, and use what you have.

> Then they asked him, "What must we do to do the works God requires?" Jesus answered, "The work of God is this: to believe in the one he has sent." (John 6:28–29 NIV)

Why? Because your choices now depend on what *you* do to secure your eternal life. You must make a personal choice, a personal decision, that you want to live now and forevermore. You want to live spiritually, mentally, and physically in the manner that has been purposed for you. You cannot do this alone. You need God. Inside you, something is missing.

I am reminded of a conversation that the Mad Hatter had with Alice in *Alice in Wonderland* by Lewis Carroll.

The Mad Hatter said to Alice, "You're not the same as you were before. You were much more muchier. You lost your muchness."

Alice responded, "My muchness?"

"In there." The Hatter pointed to her heart. "In there, something is missing."

What's missing in your core? A human is a spirit being with a soul housed in a body. I call it an "earth suit." Our spirits make us rational. When we are out of sync with our Creator, our spirit is restless. Our spirit doesn't know or remember how or what the Creator requires of us. We do and say things that we think will bring us peace and happiness. We know only by the spirit that has been regenerated in us.

> For what man knoweth the things of a man, save the spirit of man which is in him? Even so the things of God knoweth no man, but the spirit of God. (1 Corinthians 2:11)

We have been separated from the one who gives life. Sin in all forms—carelessness, stubbornness, jealousy, envy, procrastination—has created a chasm of separation. Disobedience in all forms is sin. And it is usually these feelings of loss and separation or a great trial that sends us running back to God.

> But I will call upon the Lord and He will save me. (Psalm 55:16)

There is good news. If you are a sinner and you have never confessed that Jesus is Lord, read John 3:16: "For God so loved the world that he gave his one and only Son, that whoever believes in him shall not perish but have eternal life" (NIV). And if you have accepted Him but have lost your way, read 1 John 1:9: "If we confess our sins, he is faithful and just and will forgive us our sins and purify us from all unrighteousness" (NIV).

> It's a journey, this thing called life and we really never know where it will take us or how we will arrive at that place of me. Of you. It's in the unexpected that will more than likely lead us to our purpose. God is so soverignly in charge of all things that everything that happens to us is designed in such a way that it will always serve our good. The Apostle Paul stated in (Romans 8:28), "And we know that all things

work together for good to them that love God, to them who are the called according to his purpose." The Apostle gave this encouragement to the church at Rome in that day. But this call is not the call to preach but the call to purpose.

You must decide who you want to be and what type of man or woman you want to be. What type of example will you be for others? Once that decision has been made manifest, everything else will fall into place. Once you make that decision, then the real battle for living begins. When you receive and accept the gift of the Holy Spirit, and He lands on you, something happens. You will never be the same again.

There is a way of knowing God, but the Holy Spirit allows you to *know* God and know that He has awakened something inside you—a power, a confidence, a reality that you never knew existed for you. You saw it in others, but you failed to see that you could have it too. Your treasure is being exposed. Allow what's inside you to take over, to lead and guide you. Let this newfound life that now resides in you determine the who, what, when, where, and why of your life. Let the Holy Spirit that resides in you determine your life and uncover the real, authentic you.

3

BEWARE THE POWER OF RELIGION

> And Jesus said, For judgment I am come into this world, that they which see not might see; and that they which see might be made blind.
>
> —John 9:39

This journey is a race, just as the Bible suggests. It's a race not to be won easily. In April 2005, I was struggling—struggling to learn and struggling to understand what I was to do with what the Lord had deposited within me, much of which I did not understand.

I have this treasure, and you too have a treasure deep within you. I knew it was there, but I didn't fully understand its value. The best description I can give is that it is almost was like watching the various people on *Antiques Roadshow* bring what they think might be a valuable object to be appraised. It's time for us to appraise our value.

The day my spirit heard the call, I knew I would be on a road that few travel. It would be a world that I had not seen before, a road I needed and wanted to travel, but I was afraid to travel alone. I was afraid of it, afraid to say yes, because nothing—absolutely nothing—was right.

I was clawing my way back. Nothing was as it should have been. Looking back at that scenario now, I laugh, just as Sarah laughed when God came to her and told her, in her old age, that she would conceive and bear a child. What I failed to realize was that this new thing *was* about me and *was not* about me. It was about something I did not understand, and I really didn't know if I wanted to understand. It was a continual call that came from a deep place. The worse things became, the more the call compelled me. Suddenly, I realized, *It's not about me but all about my purpose in Him.*

I heard it, yet I suppressed it, deep down in my psyche, for as long as God would allow me to do so. All the while, I thought, *What will people say? Who will take anything seriously that I have to say?* My mind was always playing with me until the Lord was ready for me or I was ready for Him.

I remember hearing, *Step into me and out of religious ideas and processes.* I, of course, did not realize that I was in "religion," in the most negative sense of the word. I had to move from religion to worship. I was in religion, yet I knew there was more. I was doing what everyone else was doing, even though I could feel that I was different. I was gripped by fear, yet thirsty for the Word to saturate my soul. I was yearning to pour out what was inside me. There was so much, and He just kept calling. I was in a church where I felt as if I could not breathe; I could not move. Raising my hand would bring on another action and reaction, and it would continue until the Holy Ghost had culminated His work. I could feel myself withering inside; my resistance was dying. I was like a withering flower that needed to be replanted, fertilized, and watered.

Our religious teachings tell us to stay at this church forever. For some of us, that works. For some, it doesn't. It all revolves around our kingdom callings. Then, there are the standard religious reasons: "If you leave, others will follow"; "You are splitting up the church"; "Husbands and wives should worship together." I heard it all, not directly to me, but I heard it all.

PERMISSION

The word *religion*, in itself, is a mystery with many definitions. From the *Oxford Dictionary*, it means "the belief in and worship of a superhuman controlling power, especially a personal God or Gods." From *Merriam-Webster*, the definition is "a personal set or institutional system of religious attitudes, beliefs and practices."

The Bible expresses religion in a way that we are able to see its effect.

> Do not merely listen to the word, and so deceive yourselves. Do what it says. Anyone who listens to the word but does not do what it says is like someone who looks at his face in a mirror and, after looking at himself, goes away and immediately forgets what he looks like. But whoever looks intently into the perfect law that gives freedom, and continues in it-not forgetting what they have heard, but doing it-they will be blessed in what they do. Those who consider themselves religious and yet do not keep a tight rein on their tongues deceive themselves, and their religion is worthless. Religion that God our Father accepts as pure and faultless is this: to look after orphans and widows in their distress and to keep oneself from being polluted by the world. (James 1:22–27 NIV)

The word is Latin in origin—*religare*, meaning "to bind." From the old French *religio*, it means "obligation, bond, reverence." For me, *Merriam-Webster*'s definition is the best fit today, in relation to who we are and what we are doing. Many of us grew up hearing and thinking that the word *religion* meant holiness or spirituality. It has confused our minds and muddled our reasons for regularly attending worship. We thought those religious folks were spiritual folks and that they actually meant what they said. Because we saw them in religious circles, we assumed that they were walking the walk and talking the talk. Oftentimes these people are doing all they can to survive. So what we see is not always how it is and then we find ourselves disappointed in these so called spiritual folk that we have looked to as examples. It's like the Pharisees, who taught one thing and did another. I call it *pharisetical* teaching. The Pharisees did not practice what they preached. Therefore do and observe everything that they command you; but do not imitate their lives, for though they tell others what to do, they do not do it themselves. (Matthew 23:3 Weymouth New Testament).

Truthfully, I didn't pay much attention in church. Mostly, I attended because my friend circle attended, and I didn't want to be left out. Our pastors preached fire and brimstone, hell and damnation. And for the longest time, I was afraid of God. I don't mean that reverential fear that our parents and grandparents spoke of, I was just plain ole scared. It was a fact; I was going to hell. In those early days, the God I knew was always mad at us. Much of that teaching did not make sense then, but it does now.

There remains some old religious hold-outs, those old teachings. I believe they were taught with the greatest of intent but not with much substance. I also believe those pastors genuinely cared about the congregation, but, for some of us, the message just did not hit home. Based on the definitions and root-word findings stated above, our method of reconnecting and rebinding has taken a turn toward the wrong lane. Religion has replaced spirituality. Religion identifies us a people who are not trying to connect or reconnect With God. Over time we have allowed our religion to cause a great separation. This separation is not based on unity but based on who we think we are—based on our material wealth, status, and education. When someone says, "I'm religious," I take that to mean they have a religious affiliation with one of the many denominations. More conversation would be needed to determine if they are simply church goers or spiritual participators.

Many of those religious practices remain embedded in my psyche even today. Practices that came from misinterpretation of the scriptures. What we call church rules could have been explained simply as rules of etiquette, such as going bare-legged, what our elders call not wearing panty hose to church or wearing pants to morning worship. These are practices that I grew up, but the funny thing is that no one could give a rational explanation for them.

Religion can be a burden, such as thinking, "My family began this church. I'm entitled"; "My house is bigger. I'm entitled"; "I tithe more. I'm entitled; "This is the way we have always done it", You get the picture. Religion leaves no room for growth or progress. Religion cannot transform us into what God wants us to be. More importantly, religion stifles our kingdom transformation.

First John 2:6 speaks of you who claim to be attached to Christ, abiding in Christ, should walk as He walked. "The one who says he abides in Him ought himself to walk in the same manner as He walked (1 John 2:6 NASB). Religion keeps us from the kingdom and holds us resistant to change; therefore, we find ourselves loyal to a system that will leave us stagnating and yearning for clarity. Religion is a system of external reactions that scream, "See me," from the outside. I can't allow you to see the real me. So I remain locked into what I know because religion has kept my mind closed to the reality of me. I go through the action of religion to suppress my fear, anger, hurt, pain, and loneliness.

I have heard people say, "I'm gonna have to lay down my religion." I have found that when most folk say this, they are "fixing to," or "getting ready," to do something that goes against what they know to be right, truthful, and the standard. They are saying that, for a minute, they are going to lay down the right standard and fight, cuss, tell you how it is. Remember it's their individual standard of what is right and just. What is actually happening is that they laid down the biblical standard of righteousness.

You may think I am someone holy and spiritual because I have learned to go through the actions of the church tenants and precepts. Because I am always on the second pew, I am always in my place. Religion has me in a holding pattern. I liken it to a plane waiting to land, circling in that confined space until the air traffic controller gives permission to enter the landing space. My religion, not my spirituality, has caused me to have a major identity crisis that even

I have a difficult time understanding. I know who I am; I just can't express it.

Religion focuses on what our eyes see versus what is happening in our hearts. Our egos swell, and we become people unable to recognize ourselves. For the sake of understanding, we serve our particular religious practices, based on the system of beliefs the religion supports, which can be directly traced to how we were raised, or who we marry, or our need at the time we joined that particular denomination.

When you compare the word *religion* up against the reason Jesus came, we find that He came not for religion but to save the world.

> For God sent not his son into the world to condemn the world: but that the world through him might be saved. John 3:17

Jesus made it clear in His teachings that going through the motions of religious duties does not give us the opportunity to understand true freedom from those religious ideas versus true liberty to serve Him in spirit and in truth and to appreciate the why of His being wrapped in flesh and coming to save us from eternal damnation. Because of who Jesus is (the Son of God), because of where He's been (to hell and Hades), and because of what He's done (He was crucified, died, was buried, and defeated death at resurrection), He has made the way for our return to Eden. He paid the ultimate cost.

As we search and try to find our way in this age of multiple generations worshipping together and searching for common ground, the one thing we should remember is that although times change, the gospel has been and will remain the same message of hope and good news. I believe if we remain true to the Word that we can accommodate all generations. If we don't navigate the waters together in unity, we will continue to put up religious walls of fear and create boundary lines where there should be freedom to move.

During this time in my life, I was feeling the pantyhose kind of angst. I was worn out and wearing myself out, Sunday after Sunday after Sunday. The manifestation preceded the decision. I could see it—really see it—happening. I had to hold my head up, straighten my shoulders, and carefully pay attention to what the Word of the Lord was revealing to me. I knew it had to be about Him and not about me. Several events and circumstances pushed me to the edge, but that isn't important to the story; there will always be people and things in your way.

The key for me was Habakkuk 2:2. The Word gave me this answer: "Write down clearly on tablets what I reveal to you, so that it can be read at a glance" (Habakkuk 2:2 Good News Translation). Just be quiet, listen, wait, pray, and meditate. I was so worried and anxious about disappointing people—what would they say? Would they accept me?

But when you hear the Lord, when you hear the call, you cannot rest until you answer Him. When you are truly called, you will understand—above all else—that your position, your mantle, is to preach the gospel to save souls. It's quite simple.

My husband could see my angst and my struggle, but I don't know that he fully understood what was going on inside of me. I had to think of my family as well. But the Lord, who is all-knowing, worked this out for me too. Nothing can stop the purpose of God. What we think of as delay is only the appointed time coming to fruition—the time for the thing to happen. Trust the process. Give yourself a chance to get caught up into what is falling on you. You will find yourself in the midst of time and purpose. They are connected.

Any process we go through will get worse before we see the light. It's dark in the process. The word *process* means that something is happening; there are more elements to this thing. And once the process takes shape, and you begin to get a taste and see—no matter how large or small or fragmented—you get caught up and you cannot turn around. You will get caught up in the power of the anointing, the power of the Shechinah glory—a true glimpse, a true taste of the heavenlies. It changes you. It's as if your insides have been rearranged. Your eyes see differently. You cease to hear with your ears and begin to hear from your spirit place. Your mind responds differently. There are moments when you wonder, *What happened?* Everything is tied up in this journey.

Again, there was that call. "I did not tell you to stay. Be where you will grow and make a difference. Your lesson was to stand. You have done that. But there are times when you will need to move to get to the next phase of the journey. If you believe in the Word and in the power of the Word, then you have the answer. If you love Him, obey Him. How you feel does not elevate the kingdom of God. You have been called you to be a builder—build. You have been called for more."

I said, "What about where I am now?"

I heard, "The congregation will not live or die because of you. You have always known that it would not be your permanent home. You know your real fear; he will be okay. As this is your chance, this will also be his chance. You have been given the permission to move. You have been called for more than what you are doing. I have called you, and humankind cannot stop you. Just obey. Be strong and of good courage, for I will be with you."

I responded, "These are the words spoken to Joshua."

The response was, "The Word transcends time and space. As they were for Joshua, so are they for you. You are released."

I remember vividly the Sunday morning when I was released, when I declared my call to preach the gospel. It was as if I was lifted and pushed out of the pew to the "chair." In the Baptist Church, the chair is a place of repentance, testimony, prayer, prayer requests, and anything that the congregant may want to express. As soon as those words were out of my lips, my hand immediately went over my mouth and I thought, *Oh Lord, what have You done?* I wanted to reach into the atmosphere, grab those words, and stuff them back into my mouth. This was the black Baptist Church, where they don't believe in female anything.

The sanctuary was dead silent. I wasn't sure what to do next; I'm sure the pastor did not know either. I felt naked in a crowd of onlookers. *Finally*, the pastor said something, although I can't remember what it was. What I do remember is that after the service, various people came up to shake my hand and make statements that I think they truly meant as support, such as "Well, I guess it's okay," and "Good luck with your preaching." Looking back, it was funny in its own way. Only the Lord knows what the Lord knows.

In May 2014, I was visiting a particular church. It was a familiar congregation—that too was another issue for me, something else I struggled with. I had been there more than once to visit. I was drawn to the anointing that was present. I wanted to be there. Those familiar questions crept up again. Could I grow there? Would I grow there? Would they accept me as a kingdom member, or would they accept me because they knew me? That lingering anointing pulled me in. The atmosphere was charged with the presence of the power of the Holy Spirit. Again, the Lord released His power to move me. The natural occurrence was filled with purpose. I didn't know that the pastor of this congregation had begun this ministry five years before I officially became a member. But God is everywhere and knows all things, and what I didn't know was that when the pastor began the ministry, my name was added to the actual charter. I learned this much later, after I became a member, and we were in the process of filing for 501C3 status. *But* the Lord.

> In their hearts humans plan their course, but the LORD establishes their steps. (Proverbs 16:9 NIV)

I shared this with you to say this: He hears you. Whatever the issue, He has worked it out for your good and His glory. Stay the course, listen, and wait. Be affirmed in knowing this.

4

WALK WITH ME

> Take my yoke upon you and learn from me, for I am gentle and humble in heart, and you will find rest for your souls.
>
> —Matthew 11:29 (NIV)

How do we begin to comprehend what God has purposed for us? We must strengthen our faith. It will take determination and persistence to bring into existence the predetermined course that has been laid out for us to follow. It is only by faith we get to where God wants us to be. We also must understand that suffering is a necessary part of our journey.

Spiritual Significance

Know who you are. If you question everything about yourself, now is the time to pursue you. There is no one like you. You are one of a kind. Celebrate you and the essence of the spirit that is within you. There are things you want to do, dreams that have not become manifest for you. It's time to become fully engaged in the purpose and promises that the Lord has created for us. There are things you want to do for yourself—do them.

Now is the time for you to come to the aide of you. Walk with the Lord, and everything—not some things; everything—that has been promised to you will come to fruition. Settle yourself.

My Response

I am learning. It has taken all these years to see me, to be true to who I am and who I want to be. This is one of the first lessons that we should teach our sons and daughters: be true to yourself. Not in an undisciplined manner, but be true to what the Lord has deposited in you. I didn't know it was there, and you may not know either. All I knew was that there was a longing, a primal cry for help. I was so covered in fear, doubt, fear, disobedience, fear, restlessness. The crux was fear. Fear will destroy your life, your hopes, your dreams, and your aspirations.

Fear speaks to our inner beings. It replaces *can* with *can't* and *should* with *shouldn't*. While all the promises of God are *yea* and *amen*, we hear the opposite. When we embrace the *yes* of God, all things fall into place, although not without setbacks or hardships. It's called process. His promises assure us that we are seen and heard (Psalm 4:3), and that we can rely on the finished work of Calvary to assure us that because He won, we too shall win.

Use your time wisely. Use it for you. Speak life to it. Asses where you want to be and where you want to go, but most of all, see who you want to be. Dissect the negative out. You are a student, a learner, a teacher, a mentor, a problem-solver, an encourager, and a supporter. You are strong and mighty in God, mighty in and with the Word. The Word penetrates and fortifies you; it feeds you, nourishes you, and sustains you.

God has the key to our purpose, and only in Him can that purpose be brought to life. Only in Him can purpose manifest its purpose. Go against the grain. You already have been preordained

PERMISSION

to be labeled peculiar, as it states in 1 Peter 2:9: "But ye are a chosen generation, a royal priesthood, an holy nation, a peculiar people; that ye should shew forth the praises of him who hath called you out of darkness into his marvelous light." Why not be that person?

Why risk failure because you don't know what you are created to do? Find where you fit in. Follow your gut. There is list of Bible witnesses who knew they were called for something; they just didn't know what that was. Moses knew he was the deliverer; he just didn't know what to do until he saw and experienced the essence of God and learned to depend on Him. Esther knew what she needed to do, and because she depended on God, she prevailed.

And then there are those who think they are one thing and come to realize that they are more. The apostle Paul was a killer, a murderer of Christians. But his experience with God on that fateful day changed his life forever. Be scared, but do it despite your fear.

You are designed to have a natural flow when you are in your purpose. There may be difficult days, but because you are working in your purpose, the mission just comes naturally. You instinctively know what to do and where to find the answer. If your purpose demands things of you that you think you can't muster, know that you are incorrect in thinking that what you are doing is coming from a place of true purpose. Purpose only pulls out of you what's in you. Purpose can't pull from you what you don't have to give. (The old folks would say that you can't squeeze blood from a turnip.) You have to work with God to release what's within you.

Everyone doesn't fit everywhere. We may attempt to fit ourselves into places and with people, but it doesn't work because it's a forced fit. Just as we outgrow clothes and shoes, we also outgrow the things and people in life that simply do not fit anymore—and we don't fit them.

Think of the times you have been with a crowd when you didn't want to be, but you succumbed to peer pressure. Your spirit was uneasy, and you were annoyed that you fell in the trap. You wonder, *Is it me?* You attempt to evaluate the situation and the associations, but you can't quite put your finger on the problem. You carry on, and these things and associations often last a lot longer than they should. You keep the jeans, although they no longer fit; the shoes are worn, and you've outgrown them. It's a struggle. You're attached to them, but you've outgrown them. It's easy to throw out the jeans; not so much the people.

What you want is an easy way out. *Maybe they will let me go, and I won't need to do anything. What is happening? What do I do? How do I find my way? How do I find my place? I just want to be me—free to serve, free to live, free to work, free to worship.* Have you ever had those thoughts?

People and situations will come in and out of your life. Then there is that one person or circumstance that saunters into your life, and you know that's where you belong. You are drawn to this essence—their speech, their teaching. It's something you know is tied to your destiny and your purpose. This is forward movement. Attempting to fit in is a crutch.

You are called to stand out. "To let your light so shine before men that they may see your good works, and glorify your father which is in heaven" (Matthew 5:16).

We have lost perception of who we are. If you don't know you, then how can you demonstrate you? Knowing *you* is the key to *you*. How can you make the difference you are called to make without knowing who you are? Therefore, you must fit with yourself first. Each test you face will set you back or shove you forward. It's up to you and how you fit. The little you know of you now is nothing compared to what is to come for you.

Remain constant and consistent. You may want to scream, but stay constant. You will cry in the midnight hour, but stay constant. You will want to quit, but stay constant. Your responsibility is to be true to who God is and to ensure that your relationship with Him is solid. Rely on Him to open the situation to you in real time because what you expect often is not how the situation really is. It's not, as we say, get in where you fit in. There is a place for you. You must be purposeful and intentional.

We must work in the present. God is a *now* God. We cannot just coast along, doing what others think we should do. That's called living in the grain. We should be going against the grain. Coasting along finds us just doing what it takes to get along—not making any waves, not opening our mouths, not using our voices, not challenging the wrongs we see or speaking any untruths.

An abundant life is not always money and stuff and things. By biblical standards, an abundant life is joy and peace and inner sanctity. If we become complacent with fitting in, all the treasure that God has deposited into us will never be found.

This book would not have come to fruition if I had chosen to be complacent and fit in. And as with all things with God, it is never too early or too late. Things happen right on time. We will never be fully self or fulfilled with self if we choose to be like Bob and do what Bob wants us to do. God is always the preeminent mentor.

Choose your friends wisely. You want the type of friendship that Jonathan and David had, or Naomi and Ruth, or Paul and Timothy. As you read their accounts, what you will learn from their encounters will be invaluable to you as you grow. These accounts represent friends who are with you because they love you and believe in you—no other reason, no ulterior motive. They are blessed because of you.

You must change the narrative of *you*. That is the reason for change. You don't want to be recognized as _____ (fill in the blank for you). God is by your side for you to lean on, in front of you to guide you, and behind you in case you fall.

5

PRIVILEGE

Train up a child in the way he should go and make sure you also go the same way.

—African proverb

I grew up in a privileged house of strong black women. Now, what you might call privilege and what I call privilege are probably two very different definitions. There were no fancy jobs, no old money, and no new money. It was more like daily work money from the efforts of my grandmother, aunt, and great-aunt being domestics (cleaning other folks' houses) and taking in ironing. And for the longest time, the iron I remember was not electric. (To this day, I hate to iron.)

I was the first baby in our family in a long time. I soon learned that I belonged to everyone but especially to my grandmother. Today, my children laugh when we are around all the cousins and hear stories of "Sissy" and how spoiled she was. Our home was the family home. Built by my great-grandfather, it's at least 150 years old. I can remember my great-grandmother, who was bedridden, dying in that house and during those days wakes were held in the living room.

The house still stands, not good but well enough for my mom, who is eighty-nine, to continue living there. I pray it holds up with our patching work for as long as she needs it. Most of the family moved away in the great migration to find a better life in various parts of the country. Kansas, Missouri, Chicago, Detroit, and California. But summers and holidays always brought them back home to the country—the South, as they called it. I think to some of them, it was like Vegas, in that they could do things at home that they couldn't do anyplace else. Our house was the first stop—smells of moth balls and cedar and always full of family and friends.

I realized early that although my mother had me, my grandmother owned me, and my aunt—my mom's twin sister—ruled me. She made the rules. My aunt died this year. Although she was mean as a snake to most, I loved her. She was my heroine. Growing up was not difficult for me. There were rules to follow, manners to mind, and a way that things were supposed to be done. I did all those things. I acted the way all good children were supposed to act because I did not want to be in trouble. I left that to my sister, who came along three years later. I never wanted for anything. I had the best clothes, shoes, and toys. Life, to me, was a breeze, but there was that underlying current of expectation.

There is a price to pay when you don't do, think, and act as everyone expects you to do. When those mannerisms, habits, and behaviors are taught at an early age, it's difficult to shake them. I knew I was loved; that was never in question. But what I grew to learn was that love has boundaries, and I was expected to stay within those boundaries. Sometimes that's good, and sometimes it's not so good. Love and unconditional love have two very different meanings. Being the firstborn often can be a handicap. It took some time for me to figure that out as well. Expectations, if not kept in perspective, can keep you from being who you really are. That lot seems to fall heavily on only children and firstborns.

PERMISSION

We did not walk around with surly attitudes. In my day—and now, as well—parents thought they created our personas. We were a reflection of our upbringing. The acknowledgments of *please* and *thank you*, the *yes ma'ams*, and the use of *Mr.* and *Mrs.* before a person's surname were signs of respect. And if that didn't happen, it was the parents' fault. If the child looked good, the parent looked good.

After the first lesson, there was a silent yet clear expectation that once you understood the lesson, there was no room for error. The children were expected to be what everyone else wanted and expected them to be—until we started to grow up. There was no "train up a child in the way that he should go"; it was more like, "I'll train her in the way I want her to be"—in the kindest sense. Expectations also create a false sense of security, a sense of being better than, although internally, you know that is not the case. Externally, however, it's how you arrive and how you are defined.

As I grew, it became a heavy load. Because if I failed to meet the expectation—well, Lord forbid. My aunt's punishment was silence. And to me there is nothing as disrespectful or demeaning as offering silence or ignoring someone as a method of punishment. So I was 99 percent what I was expected to be and 1 percent me. As a kid, that's okay. But as kids enter their formative years, if they aren't offered the freedom to express themselves and to discover what they want for themselves, I can guarantee that one day, the box will open and everyone will be shocked that they question who they are. It's funny; it took many years before I was finally able to give myself permission to be me—permission to breathe, to live, to exhale, to grow, to make mistakes, to say no, to say yes, to just be me.

Permission is a powerful word to apply to your person. Permission to move from there to here, from here to there. Please don't misunderstand; life was good for me. I would not trade my childhood for anything. There were perks to my being the favorite. Still, I was determined to do better by my children or at least to do things differently. I was determined not to smother them with a false sense of who they were. I wanted them to become the people they were meant to be. Today, I see awesome adults. God has richly blessed us, despite some of our failings. The one thing I have wanted for them is that they not think I am perfect or that I have done everything right. That's far from it because together, we have had some difficult times, but again, the Lord loved us through it.

I hope that knowing a little about me will help you to understand why giving yourself permission is crucial to an abundant life—abundant in joy, peace, happiness, goodness, kindness, and laughter. The Lord came so that we could have abundant life.

Issues keep us bogged down. Things we don't know affect us in ways we cannot understand. For example, Father's Day comes around each year on the third Sunday of June. I start dreading it right after my birthday on June 2. It wasn't until last year that I finally came face-to-face with the truth of Father's Day—my truth.

My pastor had called the night before and asked if could bring the Word to our congregation on Father's Day.

My father-in-law had recently died and I thought this would be a good Sunday to accompany him to church. My husband was having a hard time; he was not in a good place. Unresolved issues magnify grief. It was to be a surprise because normally we would be attending separate houses of worship. It was an excuse for me to skip this father's day ay my church. I called my Pastor to let him know that I would not be at morning worship.

I could tell from the phone call that he was a little irritated that I would not be at our service, he said, "Okay then. I'll just go to plan B. Sunday morning came and I felt compelled to be in attendance at my church. I knew what this day represented and I didn't want to go, but I knew it was the right thing to do.

As soon as I stood up to preach, I felt convicted. A wave of being engulfed in Spirit came over me. I came clean.

Father's Day is a holiday that I don't like. It makes me uncomfortable and uneasy. It makes me feel alone. I had father figures but not my father. It makes me feel alone because I had nothing to share. Everyone was giving tributes to their fathers with such statements as, "My dad was my hero"; "My father taught me to

PERMISSION

drive"; "My father said …" My father, my father, my father. You get the idea. I had to come clean.

I don't like this holiday because I did not have a father to offer a tribute. I knew who my father was. He came to visit when he could and called several times, but I was so mad that I became indifferent. I did not make the best of each visit or phone call. He had missed those important years of my life and my indifference would not allow me to question why. Then he became ill. We spoke on the phone some, but I don't think I realized how ill he was. And then he died.

I asked myself, over and over, if I had known how ill he was, would I have traveled to see him? I'd like to think I would have. There were not any more chances to forgive and forget. Children often only know one side of the husband-and-wife narrative. And then, after a while, they just accept what is or isn't and carry on. My father ended each phone call with "I love you."

Father's Day makes us remember, whether we want to or not, how it really is, and then we must deal with what is left. I needed my father, and at sixty-two years old, I still needed him. But as soon as I released the pain, I felt I could breathe.

Girls and boys, men and women, all equally need their fathers. Remember I told you about those strong women in my family, and they were. But women cannot give what the presence of a father brings to a family. It's simply how God intended it to be, and anything else is just less than that.

As I began to study the Word more and more, I saw that I was less angry over what I didn't get but more so for what I'd missed. On that Father's Day Sunday, I could not speak of my father teaching me to drive a car, being at my graduation, or being there for the birth of my children—all those important life moments. His absence did not negate what I did have, but still, it was a missing part of me. Father's Day brings out that missing part of me, and I despised the feeling.

Fathers have a way of speaking that brings about a sense of completeness and confidence. They admonish and correct and carry the weight of the family in a way that women cannot. I believe that those of us who did not have a father present, or if he was present but wasn't so good at being a father, are left with a huge void, with unsettled issues, and with a knowledge of not knowing who we are. But I also believe that we can put those feelings and issues in a place where we are able to overcome. Because at the end of the day, all children want, no matter their ages, are their parents. Children want to know that their mom and dad—good, bad, or indifferent—are there for them.

Lesson: If you have parents, be grateful, for without them, you would not be the *you* that you are. In whatever way you are here, it's because of that union. And make no mistake in your thinking—God gave you exactly the parents you were supposed to have, the parents He ordained for you. You were purposed for your parents. I still feel the emptiness but knowing that he is with God and knowing that God is with me eases the loss.

I can remember the times he called, the letters he wrote, the cards he sent, and the visits he made. And for that, I am grateful.

6

YOU CAN CHANGE

And be not conformed to this world: but be ye transformed by the renewing of your mind, that ye may prove what is that good, and acceptable, and perfect, will of God.

—Romans 12:2

There are some scriptures that just stop you in your tracks—those meaty ones that make you say whoa! Even before I knew anything about the apostle Paul, I had the above scripture. Took me some time to understand what it was saying (remember the Word lives and breathes), but I knew this was me.

The expression of Romans 12:2 is explained best by Kenneth S. Wuest and gives so much light to the words.

> And stop assuming an outward expression that does not come from within you and is not representative of what you are in your inner being but is patterned

after this age, but change your outward expression to one that comes from within and is representative of your inner being, by the renewing, resulting in your putting to the test what is the will of God, the good and well-pleasing and complete will, and having found that it meets specifications, place your approval upon it. (Kenneth S. Wuest, *Word Studies from the Greek New Testament*)

And from the Message Bible:

Don't become so well adjusted to your culture that you fit into it without even thinking. Instead, fix your attention on God. You'll be changed from the inside out. Readily recognize what He wants from you, and quickly respond to it. Unlike the culture around you, always dragging you down to its level of immaturity, God brings the best out of you, develops well-formed maturity in you. (Romans 12:2)

There is a natural proclivity to go along with what the world is doing. Going along, however, often doesn't match up with what we know to be true in our souls.

People say you can't teach an old dog new tricks; the Bible calls it putting new wine in old wine skins. I put my trust in the Bible. I believe we can change our thinking, which will change our actions, which will transform our lives in ways we can only imagine. But until we know, we don't know.

We are not our bad decisions or our bad choices. There is a plan, a purpose, for you and me. When we don't know ourselves and when who we thought we were is not being lived out, we walk in confusion and turmoil. When we don't know ourselves and some trauma or decision does not produce the outcome we expected, it leaves a hole in our souls. And here comes that silent scream that no one hears but you.

Our insides are like Jell-O—never still, constantly on the move. Reminds me of the professor in the holiday classic *Frosty the Snowman*. "Busy, busy, busy." If we stay busy, we don't have time to think about or try to change what's wrong—until we crash.

Laughter but no joy.

Company but no real friends.

Rest but no peace.

You are not giving *you* a chance to step into purpose.

My pastor has a saying: "Life is hard. You have to live it hard." These words are so true. There is a huge chasm between where I come from, where I am, and where I am purposed to be. I have been separated from my purpose. Whether intentionally or unintentionally, it happened. I lost my way. I forgot who I am and where I came from. But maybe I never knew.

When we are in that place, we can go to John 1:5: "The light shines in darkness and the darkness comprehend it not." Another power scripture. I first understood this to mean that darkness does not understand the light. What it really says is that darkness can never overcome light. His light reveals to us His love and His purpose for us. His light opens our eyes and dispels the darkness. It gives us clarity and revelation. His light lets me see me and you see you. But for the light—I believe that light seeks us out. I know that may be hard to understand and it's hard to explain, but there are mysteries we don't yet understand, and I believe this is one of them.

I believe that because God loves you and me so much, He doesn't want any of us to perish. I believe that we have this place within us, and when we are in those dark places, the light seeks us out, by a sound, a word—something to remind us that He is there.

If there is to be a change in who you are or what you are going to do, all things must be in order for the change. I don't mean in an organized order. A shift occurs when something disturbs the normal process or you receive new information that would change the way you understand an issue. A shift is nothing more than change. When you shift, something must change, and if it doesn't change, you have not shifted.

Everything can be wrong, but the wrong things aligned together can cause a shift. The shift can be large or small, but something must change. Revelation of the Word should cause a shift. Remember that sudden moment I spoke about? It aligns along the fault line that is about to shift. The sudden shift will cause a change in the landscape of your life—a change in your actions and responses. It's almost as if *suddenly* is speaking to you, forcing you to make a much-needed change of direction or thought. *Suddenly* ushers in the new paradigm.

The Word of God lives.

> For God's message is full of life and power, and is keener than the sharpest two-edged sword. It pierces even to the severance of soul from spirit, and penetrates between the joints and marrow, and it can discern the secret thoughts and purposes of the heart. (Hebrews 4:12 Weymouth New Testament)

That is *power*. It is so powerful that it is able to know and expose what is in our hearts. It comforts us, berates us, and knows us. The Word becomes you as you continue to be intimate with it. The Word, if and when you apply it, convicts you, intimidates you, and drives you to become.

How I wish that someone had shared this with me, years ago. I cannot emphasize enough how important the Word is to our becoming whole; how necessary it is that the Bible be our source for answers; how vital it is to study and meditate and study and meditate. As you do this, you will begin to receive answers to the questions, and revelation will come to those areas that lie hidden. Light will shine in the darkness.

It can happen suddenly, or it can be a long wait. Listen for change. Watch for change so that when it happens, you will know what to do; so that as the change occurs, you will know that you are in the midst of something big. It's like an earthquake. Sometimes earthquake warnings can alert us, but at other times, that the warning signal is not strong enough, and that sudden quake hits. You will be in the midst of change.

Again, I heard in my spirit,

> You have some understanding, but you have not been given the full scope. Hear the Word, and look for Him in everything and everywhere. Remember the omniscience, the omnipresence, and omnipotence of God. It is that knowledge of Him and that knowledge that you can do it that will keep you striving for more, for God. Remember it's all about the new knowledge that causes the old paradigm to change. You must learn who you are in Him to survive the shift.
>
> From the foundations of the world, you have been called, but you were not able to hear. You could not comprehend. You worked in darkness until it happened to you. It is the unsettled things. He was with you, but you did not see or hear Him because you were in the way. You are the one who slowed your progress. And now that you have seen and heard, things become clearer.

In my spirit, I sensed change. Something was happening, materially and spiritually. I am reminded that at different times and at different stages of our lives, we must have change in order to survive. As our lives go through sequences, time keeps coming around and around, and oftentimes, something comes around with which we did not identify, and we get another chance to step into it. There is time. Those days are like jump-starts. There was a day like that for me, and I thought, *Today is a perfect day for this to happen.*

The snow fell. It was nice and quiet in the house. The fireplace was on, but my mind was full of clutter. A vital step to becoming who you are destined to be is to understand why clutter is a problem. Clutter does not mean that the house is not clean. Clutter says there is a bunch of stuff in the way of what you are looking for. My spirit said, "I want you to focus. Really look at what is shown to you. See the beginning of the vision. You have seen a partial view, but you must see it all to move forward. Others will go in half knowing, but not you. You have been set apart to know what your role will be."

As we speak about change and transformation, it's apparent that we don't know enough about the subject as change seems to be on the attributes that we often fight against. It is easier to stay where we are than to do anything or be a part of anything that would push us to change or push us forward.

The past is comfortable. Even when the past is bad, you know what's there and what to expect. Moving forward is scary. It's like a little one learning to walk. I asked the Lord to expose me to *me* so that I might see me. So that I might see any pride, selfishness, and ugliness that may be in me. We cannot illuminate His glory if there is ugliness in us. We cannot serve with anything but a clean and contrite heart. This, He sees.

There was a time when I was in crisis. I don't think I understood that I could not fix anything or do anything. It was just one of those times that I had to get through. I was in a sad season—a season of regret, loss, and tears. I did not like it because I am a count-it-all-joy kind of girl. But I just could not control the season. I was reminded of another saying from my friend: "I am not living the life I sing about in my song." (It's a line from a gospel hymn by Mahalia Jackson.)

My spirit again spoke,

> You will. The promise to you is that joy will come again. There are some things that you can do, and there are issues that only God is authorized to do, things that only God holds the full authorization to resolve. I only need you to focus on you. Remember that things always look worse before they get better. Man attempts to resolve many issues of life, and God

is left out of the solution. God is the solution. You must be consistent on purpose. It is not for you to do anything except what the Word instructs you to do. If you keep your assignment, the promise will surely come to pass. But know that even if you fail, the promise is sure.

7

WARFARE

Be alert and of sober mind. Your enemy the devil prowls around like a roaring lion looking for someone to devour. Resist him, standing firm in the faith, because you know that the family of believers throughout the world is undergoing the same kind of sufferings. And the God of all grace, who called you to his eternal glory in Christ, after you have suffered a little while, will himself restore you and make you strong, firm and steadfast.

—1 Peter 5:8–10 (NIV)

It began with a dream.

In my dream, a lady was sitting at a table, looking very smug and eating a sausage sandwich. I don't know why I remembered so vividly what she was eating, but she had a look on her face that said, "I'm in charge. I've got this." Almost a challenging stare. I could not discern who she was, but she was very secure in herself.

She had a comfortable and conceited stare, a cold stare. A stare that challenged and spoke to me that said, "Who are you, and what can you do about it? I'm in your house, and I have seated myself with you, and in all the areas of your life that are causing you trouble."

It was not one thing but several things that were out of order during this time. It was a direct challenge issued at me. I got that feeling in the pit of my stomach, even in this dream state. I realized I was looking the adversary in the face. That old and ancient enemy, the devil, was goading me, daring me to do anything—daring me to move, daring me to fight, and daring me to call on the name that is above all names, daring me to pray to the one who could fight this battle for me.

Literally there were times that I felt the devil as paralyzing me, he knew I was tired, and he knew I was tired of the fight. He knew I was tired of praying and asking and not seeing any positive results. I didn't care because I was tired, but my soul cried out for me when I could not.

In the next scene there were men and women around a table of twelve, discussing how best to attack the problem. Each person had a thought, idea, or reaction as to what they thought the issue was and how to resolve it. It was an odd scene, a dark scene, a scene that said we don't have the answers; we don't know what to do. It was as if they were powerless, and they were contemplating going to the dark side to find the answers. This was another pit-of-the-stomach moment. But then, my spirit spoke: "You are not wrestling with flesh and blood but against principalities, against powers, against the rulers of the darkness of this world, against spiritual wickedness in high places."

The actual scripture of Ephesians 6:12 reads, "For we wrestle not against flesh and blood, but against principalities, against powers, against the rulers of the darkness of this world, against spiritual wickedness in high places."

I wasn't scared; I was tired. As the old folks say, *tired of being tired*. I knew the Word of God, and I knew what to do. But being tired begets being tired. I had a lot going on that I was trying to deal with of my own power. I finally managed to wake up. I knew what to do. I'd known all along. My senses had been dulled because I was so tired.

I wondered if, like Daniel, my prayers were being delayed. Had I not been diligent in my prayers? I remembered that I had prayed every day, but did I really pray or just talk? I know talk is communication, but tough times call for consistent and persistent prayer. I knew from reading Daniel that my prayer, once stated, immediately reached heaven.

Warfare is real. Know how to fight. Each attack we face is not about us, specifically; it's about who we are to the Lord. It's about our access to Him, our devotion to Him. If the devil can keep us tired and can shut down our sound, this interferes with our prayers as the answer falls down from heaven. This is why it is so important that we follow the strategic plan of the Bible.

Remember that the devil and one-third of the angels were thrown out of heaven, and he has a strategy to pull us away from God. The devil knows how much God loves us and that God will do anything for us as we confess our love for the Son He sent to save us. The devil hates us and is jealous of us. The enemy, the devil, cares nothing for us. As long as we brood over an issue, continue to cry about it, and stress over it, he will continue to bring it to our faces.

The enemy only cares about our future. He knows that his sentence has already been pronounced to hell, and he wants us to be sentenced there too. He doesn't have a way out, but we do. He wants our purpose. The enemy knows that he can *never* enter heaven again. That is a privilege that only humankind will be afforded.

I heard the word *relentless*. *Webster's Dictionary* defines the word as "showing or promising no abatement of severity, intensity, strength or pace. Unrelenting pressure." Its synonyms are dogged, unyielding, and determined. In the etymology dictionary, it is defined as hard-nosed, following a scent. I like this one; it made me laugh. In my imagination, I could see Satan following the scent of humankind, relentlessly pursuing us; relentless in his pursuit to steal, kill, and destroy—and in that exact biblical order.

He is a stealer of souls, of dreams, and of purpose. He has no other thought or plan but to continue to devise schemes to trap humankind. We must remember that we serve the Lord with the mind, and what we feed the mind determines how our minds will respond to any given situation. This is one of those hard lessons that takes a moment to digest, just don't ponder on it too long.

> And be not conformed to this world: but be ye transformed by the renewing of your mind, that ye may prove what is that good, and acceptable and perfect will of God. (Romans 12:2)

The mind is the place of reasoning and understanding. It has to be fed. Once your mind is settled, things will fall into place. I had to fix my mind on what was being revealed to me regarding this book. My spirit said that this was not the first time he would interfere, nor would it be the last. Remember the words that have been spoken to you. I am always here; keep My Word close.

Things around me are always changing. Many situations and reactions have brought me to this place and time. I was directed to 1 Peter 1:13, which says, "Wherefore gird up the loins of your mind, be sober, and hope to the end for the grace that is to be brought unto you at the revelation of Jesus Christ." You and I must look into our purpose with intention. Our purpose can be a stronghold if it is not released properly. Our purpose has to be defined by scripture, by God's Word to us. He alone is the instigator of the purpose. We observe with our eyes, but the Word must become revelation, and revelation comes via the Holy Spirit.

> But when he, the Spirit of truth, comes, he will guide you into all the truth. He will not speak on his own; he will speak only what he hears, and he will tell you what is yet to come. (John 16:13 NIV)

PERMISSION

Revelation is about God's being real to us in a way that we can change, real in a way that we will want to change because we see Him. You and I must find ourselves in the scripture and that means finding our truth within the word we have read. What is my truth? From which place am I making decisions? What is the will of God concerning me? Am I moving in the right direction? Transformation and progress are about you and me and the manner in which we want to live. No one can tell you how to do *you* or to be *you*. It must be revealed to you first so that you can manifest the truth of who you are and what you have been called to do. One of my truth scriptures—and I have several, but the one I rely on, the one that holds me up, pushes me, and says I can make it—is from the book of James:

> Consider it pure joy, my brothers and sisters, whenever you face trials of many kinds, because you know that the testing of your faith produces perseverance. Let perseverance finish its work so that you may be mature and complete, not lacking anything. (James 1:2–3)

I am learning to walk in a way that exemplifies true peace and completeness, which is not determined by what is happening around me. Don't interrupt the process, as you want to be fully developed, whole, lacking nothing, and wanting nothing. The complete New Testament commentary by Warren Wiersbe states it like this: immature people are always impatient; mature people are patient and persistent. Impatience and unbelief usually go together, just as faith and patience do (*The Wiersbe Bible Commentary*).

Mind your business and know your Word so that when you are confronted with an issue or presented with a gospel truth, you will be prepared to defend. As you allow the Word to fill you, something happens. The right scripture can convict you and bring you to tears. It can stop you right where you stand because in that scripture, you saw *you*. You will ask the Lord, "What do I do, and how shall I do it?" The Word must take hold of you and grip you so there is no escape. Are you ready?

Warfare is real. I don't speak about it a lot because I think we give Satan too much credit for ruining our lives when it's really the bad choices we've made. But make no mistake: he's out there, and he's real. That's why we must be scholars of the Word. We must adjust and adhere our lives to following the Word. The Bible leaves us a strategic plan to follow in 2 Corinthians 10:5 to overcome the power of a thought—those imaginations that deceive us and those things that stop us in our tracks and freeze us to the truth. Fear is real. Remember that fear is a spirit, but we can overcome by "casting down imaginations, and every high thing that exalteth itself against the knowledge of God, and bringing into captivity every thought to the obedience of Christ" (2 Corinthians 10:5).

It is a fight, but we have the mind of Christ; therefore, we are able to control and master the situation to His will. God's people do not have the luxury or time to give fear a stronghold. We must own up to who we are and to what crisis or trauma has happened so that we are able to walk upright again.

Transparency

Too often, those of us who are called don't walk in transparency. To be transparent means that we are honest with those we serve. We allow them to see us. Yes, there are boundaries, but we allow them to see the me that I am and the you that you are. People need to know that we are real, that we have had real pain, real agony, real struggles, real disappointments, and real mistakes and that we overcame them to walk in real joy, real peace, real strength, and real successes, and we are able to share those with a dying world. People do not have much hope in those who walk in arrogance and pride. These are the vices that inhibit a real connection with people.

A long time ago, I read *The Velveteen Rabbit* by Margery Williams. The following excerpt from the book really stood out to me:

PERMISSION

The skin horse had lived longer in the nursery than any of the others. He was so old that his brown coat was bald in patches and showed the seams underneath, and most of the hairs in his tail had been pulled out to string bead necklaces. He was wise, for he had seen a long succession of mechanical toys arrive to boast and swagger, and by and by break their mainsprings and pass away, and he knew they were only toys, and would never turn into anything else. For nursery magic is very strange and wonderful, and only those playthings that are old and wise and experienced like the Skin Horse understand all about it." What is REAL?" asked the Rabbit one day, when they were lying side by side near the nursery fender, before Nana came to tidy the room. "Does it mean having things that buzz inside you and a stick-out handle?" Real isn't how you are made," said the Skin Horse. "It's a thing that happens to you. When a child loves you for a long, long time, not just to play with, but REALLY loves you, then you become real. "Does it hurt?" asked the Rabbit. "Sometimes," said the Skin Horse, for he was always truthful. "But when you are real, you don't mind being hurt." "Does it happen all at once, like being wound up," he asked, "or bit by bit?" It doesn't happen all at once," said the Skin Horse. "You become. It takes a long time. That's why it doesn't happen often to people who break easily, or have sharp edges, or who have to be carefully kept. Generally, by the time you are real, most of your hair has been loved off, and your eyes drop out and you get loose in the joints and very shabby. But these things don't matter at all, because once you are real you can't be ugly, except to people who don't understand. "I suppose you are real?" said the Rabbit. And then he wished he had not said it, for he thought the Skin

> Horse might be sensitive. But the Skin Horse only smiled. "The boy's uncle made me real," he said. "That was a great many years ago; but once you are real you can't become unreal again. It lasts for always.

The thing I understood was that life can take a toll on us. We start out one way and end up another. The issues of life can set us back for years. Life's issues and trials change the way we act and change our physical appearances, even to the point that we may be unrecognizable. But love is enough to bring us back, even if we are on our deathbed. This is why it is so important that we have insight into ourselves. We must come to know ourselves in an intimate way.

We only become real by the struggles we have overcome, by carrying our own crosses and recognizing what the Lord has done. Often, it takes more than one struggle for us to see where we are going and that we need to turn around. As we learn to carry our own crosses, we learn to trust Jesus and build our faith so that, in the end, there is no question as to who brought us out. Being real means that we have seen some things and done some things. Being real is a process. It does not happen overnight. But while we are going through the process, we can remember that the great King David wrote, "I had fainted, unless I had believed to see the goodness of the LORD in the land of the living" (Psalms 27:13).

I would have surely lost my forever, had I not believed the Lord was my only hope and my only promise in this life and the life to come. We cannot faint or lose heart when trouble comes.

In my heart, I am an introvert. It is important, in what I am called to do, that I do not appear cold and standoffish. I think a lot, so it's important that I don't ignore people with whom I am in close contact. I'm quiet. It's important that I remain approachable because all another person has of me is his or her perception of me.

Our responses and senses in the natural can oftentimes give us a false sense of security and cause us to exhibit a lackadaisical approach toward what we see, feel, and hear. I have previously told you about the battle we face. Let me remind you that a prepared scheme has been devised in another realm for our minds, our purpose, and our very destiny. If we are not careful, we will tend to minimize and forget that we live between two worlds, heaven and earth.

The battle continues twenty-four hours a day, seven days a week. Our senses and responses, when we come from a negative place, cause emotions that steal our progress. We begin to function from a place of feeling and emotion and not from that knowledge-of-the-kingdom perspective. I cannot stress this enough. We are never as vulnerable as when we allow our emotions to supersede the power of the Word and our prayer life.

The Bible states that when the enemy comes in like a flood, "the spirit of the Lord will lift a standard against him" (Isaiah 59:19). Whatever and wherever the enemy may be—enemies at home, at work, at school, and even at church; personal enemies, private enemies, and enemies we didn't know we had. Himself, the Lord of hosts shall step in and check them. The enemy hinders the Word. He stirs us up and irritates our flesh until it rises above our spirits, and then we boil over. These emotions overtake us, and we succumb to the flesh. We act out, fighting ourselves.

8

THE END IS JUST THE BEGINNING

> Those things, which ye have both learned, and received, and heard, and seen in me, do:
> —Philippians 4:9

As the story ends, and as we sit and ponder our lives and attempt to reason things out, I find that despite the hard times, I have learned some things. I wonder if you can identify.

1. I have recognized that I have not completed everything that the Lord has laid on my heart to accomplish.
2. I have learned that life is a vapor, just as the great King Solomon stated, and that John 12:40 confirms that we all have an appointment—ready or not.
3. I have learned that as I gain knowledge of the kingdom, I have a responsibility to lead the way for others to follow. Because to whom much is given, much is required as states in Luke 12:48.

4. I have learned that separation is difficult. It alienates you. People don't understand who you are, nor are they willing to accept you as you are. Many don't want to see you succeed. You chose life, and they may not be ready for that choice. We must count the cost. (Luke 14:28).
5. I have learned that compromise is fear lying in wait (1 Chronicles 28:20).
6. I have learned that we all have a choice. Choice is what brought humankind to the place we are in this present age (Joshua 24:15).
7. I have learned that even in the most difficult of times and in the darkest of places, life is worth living. That's our job; spread the Word (John 10:10).
8. I have learned that procrastination produces waste and anxiety (Ephesians 5:15–17).
9. I have learned and continue to learn that only what you and I do for Christ will remain (Matthew 6:33).
10. I have learned that change begins first with me. I am the example; I am the story (Romans 12:2).

Go forward in love and grace. Apply what you have learned and redeem the time.

We will remember that no weapon formed against us will prosper (Isaiah 54:17).

We will remember that God is for us (Romans 8:31).

We will remember that new wine (new thoughts, new ideas) cannot be poured into old wineskins (old thought processes) (Mark 2:22).

We will remember that the name of the Lord is a strong tower (Proverbs 18:10).

We will remember that You, God, change not. You are the same as yesterday, today, and tomorrow (Hebrews 13:8).

We will remember that You, God, knew us before we were born. You ordained our lives. You knew our inward parts—our hearts, our souls, and our minds. You knew our names (Jeremiah 1:5).

We will remember that when we call God, He will answer (Jeremiah 33:3).

We will remember that to win, we must stay in the race and follow the rules (2 Timothy 2:5).

We will remember that of our strength, we have none, but with Him, all things are possible (Philippians 4:13).

We will remember that we overcome by the blood of the Lamb and the word of our testimony (Revelation 12:11).

And we end with love because *love* is the beginning and the *end*. Love is the reason we are here, and love is the reason we will continue to be. Love is the thing, the Spirit that says, "I am always with you."

Do I have regrets? Of course, but I do not live with them. They are memories from another day and time that I have learned to cherish. I have a meaning for the acronym REGRET: Release Every Goading Response Envying Truth. Feel free to make one for yourself because when the memories start to flood the memory bank, I want to focus on what regret did for me—how it grew me, loved me, and stayed with me. It helped me to overcome me and helped me to know that I am stronger and wiser than I ever thought or knew.

And this is exactly what regret is supposed to do—to bring you to you. I have nothing to complain about. Regret brought me to Matthew 6:33: "But seek ye first the kingdom of God, and his righteousness; and all these things shall be added unto you." Because of His great love for me, all I need is embedded in this scripture. He has loved me with an unconditional love, a love that allows me to be free, to walk in liberty and truth, and to be the best version of me that I can be—first for God, then for me, and then for my family. I believe there is a biblical response for every issue that we may encounter. And I believe that just as satan has schemes and strategies to derail us from our purposes, that God too has a plan for our life. His word confirms to us that very thing in (Ephesians 1:11, Good News Translation)" All things are done according to God's plan and decision; and God chose us to be his own people in union with Christ because of his own purpose, based on what he had decided from the very beginning." I believe that if we search the scriptures and then apply those precepts to the issue that we are struggling with, that the answer will be revealed to us. This means that there is a certain amount of self-work that we must engage in.

That self-work begins with prayer and meditation. These two principles will establish our relationship with God and help us to reconnect with God through words, moans and groans that are revealed in and through us by the Holy Spirit. The stronger our prayer life the stronger our connection to God. The stronger our prayer life the stronger our faith. Our faith drives our prayer life. We believe so we ask. The best of times and the worst of times calls for prayer.

There is a certain situation recorded in the Gospels of Matthew and Mark. It records the disciples attempt to expel a demon. They were unable to get the job done. Along comes Jesus and expels the demon from the young man of the demon. The disciples asked "why couldn't we drive it out?" Jesus responded "Howbeit this kind goeth not out but by prayer and fasting."(Matthew 17:21) And from (Mark 9:29), "and he said unto them, this kind can come forth by nothing, but by prayer and fasting."

There are certain situations in life that require intense prayer and fasting. Not to say that God will not or cannot perform a miracle with a simple word. He can. But this type of prayer and fasting gives us power as well. You must have faith for the fight. Prayer and fasting are spiritual disciplines that must be integrated in our lives as a lifestyle.

I too at times have been guilty of having a poor or lacking prayer life even though I feel like I am constantly conversing with God. There is a difference in these conversations vs. on my knees or in my closet prayer and supplications. In these prayers I pour out everything. These prayers may start out ugly and end up with my soul in peace knowing there is a resolution on the horizon because he paid attention to me. As in the book of Exodus, Israel was in a bad situation. But while in crisis they sought the Lord. The Bible records in (Exodus 2:23 NIV), Years passed, and the king of Egypt died. But the Israelites continued to groan under their burden of slavery. They cried out for help, and their cry rose up to God.

This is what happens, our prayers ascend to heaven. Whatever the burden and when the situation is so dire, this is the type of prayer that gets results. Purposeful prayer.

This thing called life is a journey of purpose and it continues on until we take that last earthly breath. Then, for those of us who say *yes* and surrender, life will begin anew because everything God did was *just for us*. I wonder: what if I hadn't gone back to church, back to God? What if I had continued without Him? I don't know that I can adequately answer that. I know that with each trial that has come my way, there was a peace and confidence in knowing that God was with me. I know that when I thought I was alone, I was not. I know that I cannot know—nor do I want to know—what life would have been like without Him had I not recognized that I needed Him. I feel like I was loved back to life by many people. But that's my story, and this book has shown me that I am not finished. I do not know what the next task will be, but I am ready.

He loved us to life, how powerful. In love, there is no explanation or comprehension of width, height, depth, or length. The apostle Paul prayed for the Christians at Ephesus

> For this reason I bow my knees to the Father of our Lord Jesus Christ, from whom the whole family in heaven and earth is named, that He would grant you, according to the riches of His glory to be strengthened with might through His Spirit in the inner man, that Christ may dwell in your hearts through faith; that you being rooted and grounded in love, may be able to comprehend with all the saints what is the width and length and depth and height, to know the love of Christ which passes knowledge; that you may be filled with all the fullness of God. (Ephesians 3:14–19)

Love cannot be measured because its beginning is God, and God is limitless. You cannot be separated from it because what God created, He loves eternally. It is not so limited in width that you would fall out of its parameters, even from the far corners of the world. Love's height is as limitless as the heavens and beyond. Its depth has no comparison to the deepest ocean. It is not so limited in length that it cannot reach down and grab you, no matter how far you may have fallen. God only sees you in *love*. Your sinful actions are pardoned because of the love that brings about repentance. He sacrificed His Son for you and me because of *love*.

> Above all, love each other deeply, because love covers over a multitude of sins. (1 Peter 4:8 NIV)

You see, we are commanded to love. Love is so powerful.

Love is the substance of John 3:16. What if God had not loved us back to Himself? Think of those you love in the natural. Are you able to love as God did—unconditionally? Love is the way back for all of us.

> Love is patient, love is kind. It does not envy, it does not boast, it is not proud. It does not dishonor others, it is not self-seeking, it is not easily angered, it keeps no record of wrongs. Love does not delight in evil but rejoices with the truth. It always protects, always trusts, always hopes, and always perseveres. Love never fails. (1 Corinthians 13:4–8)

> Love is the only way to grasp another human being in the uttermost core of his personality. No one can become fully aware of the very essence of another human being unless he loves him. By his love he is enabled to see the essential traits and features in the beloved person; and even more, he sees that which is potential in him, which is not yet actualized.

PERMISSION

Furthermore by His love, the loving person enables the beloved person to actualize these potentialities. By making him aware of what he can be and what he should become, he makes the potentialities come true. (Viktor E. Frankl, *Man's Search for Meaning, page 111-112, 2006 print edition*, published by Beacon Press, Boston)

I pray that as the journey continues, you and I will be instruments or vessels for the kingdom, that our hidden treasures will be revealed for all to see, that God may be glorified through us, and that we may be lights to our families, our friends and acquaintances, and any sinner who walks this world, looking for a reprieve and second chance.

The answer: love conquers all. *Amor Omnia Vincit.*

Be blessed, y'all.

AFTERWORD

As I was attempting to complete this manuscript and get it to the publisher, three things happened: My mother had been a dialysis patient. This past year, her health began to deteriorate. She died on February 7, 2020.

The second thing that happened was that while preparing and planning a funeral, I found myself in the midst of the worldwide COVID-19 pandemic. This pandemic has brought the world and many of its systems to a halt. I was stressed and pushed to the max. I was preparing to contact the publishing house and delay this manuscript. I truly felt like I was falling into a black hole. I contacted the publishing company and explained the issues in an attempt to weigh my options. But once I hung up the phone, my spirit spoke:

> Who did you consult? You were not asked or instructed to halt the process. The things you are dealing with have nothing to do with the book. The book is to help someone overcome the issues of the world in a manner that pushes God to the forefront of the problem.

As I processed this information, an unexplainable peace engulfed me, one I did not fully understand. Then, the third thing happened. The manuscript for the book was complete, for all intents and purposes. There were no more pages to add. I had found a stopping place and stopped. Yet as I was compiling the final frames for the manuscript, I found a document that was hidden in the pages of another book—pages in a handwriting I didn't recognize. When I first looked at it, I almost threw it away because I didn't know what it was. The writing was all bunched together and did not make any sense.

But after a closer look, I realized it was pages of affirmations and quotations. As I read them, I thought, *These are good readings—positive readings.* And then I realized I had read some of them and heard them from other sources. I surmised this was work my sister saved from when she was in prison and that she had held onto these pages. I have no memory of how the writings came into my possession, but I knew it was her penmanship.

I tried to separate each line to find the beginnings and endings of the quotes so that I could find the author of each quote. Technology is amazing. I have attached the pages in her handwriting with the correct credit given. She must have read these many times to find the comfort she was looking for.

It was December 12, 2007. I was sitting at my desk at work.

My son called. "Mom, have you heard about Aunt Lib?"

I responded, "No, what's going on?" I had just seen her the day before.

"I heard she's been shot, and she's dead."

Something in my stomach sank. "What do you mean?"

"Let me find out," he said. "I'll call you back."

As I set the phone down, my mom called me. I yelled, "I'm on my way to get you!"

I drove as fast as I could to pick up my mom and drive to the hospital.

Mama kept saying, "I hope she's okay. Do you think she's dead?"

Something in me knew that she was dead—my son's voice, the feeling in the pit of my stomach.

We arrived at the hospital and were taken directly to a family room. In the room were my mom, stepdad, nieces, and my husband.

The doctor came in and said, "I'm sorry. She's dead from a gunshot wound to the abdomen."

I don't remember much else, just a lot of screaming by my nieces. I left the room.

It seems the local police were apprehending a convict and gunfire ensued. My sister had been taking lunch to my nieces, and a bullet hit her. We were sure it was one of the officers' bullets.

Of course, there was an investigation, and the local authorities followed their protocols and processes. We knew what the outcome would be, and we also knew the local police would never take responsibility. It's public record. The officers were never charged with her death and were later back on the job. The convict they'd been chasing was charged with her death.

We reached out to several attorneys. One took the case but hit a brick wall with regard to any type of charge of negligence. There was no justice for her death.

As I write this, I am not sure why I was directed to add this to the manuscript. It's certainly not what I wanted to do. This was an awful time, a rough time. My sister spent time in prison on drug-related charges. She and my baby sister were very close, and to this day, she struggles. They both grew up, going to church. They knew the Lord and what He represents, but the lifestyle they lived did not always represent what they knew of the Lord. I mention this to say that I really struggled when Mama would ask me, "Where do you think Lib is?"

One day, I was standing in my living room, and I heard, as clear as day, my sister say, "Sissy, don't forget about me." I looked for her, but I could not find her in the room. Five words. I heard them, but I could not find the source. I sat down and cried. All through the process of her death and burial, I don't think I cried. I can't remember crying.

For years, Mama would ask, out of the blue, "Do you think she is cold in the ground?" I would try to explain that only her earth suit was in the ground; she was not there. She would then ask, "Do you know where she is? Can you tell me?" I was challenged by her questions and challenged to find answers that would adequately answer her questions in a way that she would understand and find comfort in. I would get so angry when she would repeatedly ask those questions over and over. I realized it was because at that time I could not adequately answer her questions. But one day the answer finally came.

The lesson I learned during this time is that we are not taught enough about the process of death and dying. It's a natural occurrence that is as important as living. We don't have one without the other. They rely on each other for us to come to our full purpose. A certain pastor and I have a recurring debate on the biblical statement of Luke 23:42–43: "And he said unto Jesus, Lord, remember me when Thou comest into Thy kingdom. And Jesus said unto him, Verily I say unto thee, today shalt thou be with me in Paradise."

To me, it is very simple. Whenever and wherever Jesus went, so shall the thief be also. I believe that all of us are fearfully and wonderfully made. I believe that God made no mistakes in creation. I believe that man is capable of the impossible. I believe there are inherent qualities that reside in us –those things that exist inside us that cannot be separated from our essential make-up. Therefore, I believe that we have a place within us, a secret place that resides in us that lies undetected. It's a place that no medical exam has found. No CT, MRI, or ultrasound can detect it. It's there. It's a place that only God knows. A place in us, that God gave us so that even in the last seconds of our earthly life we are able to commune with him only. It's a place in us that lives as we are dying and that is able to meet with God and resolve those ungodly things that we have done.

Does that mean that everyone near death will access that place? I don't know. I only know that one has to ask for repentance and forgiveness is yours because God wants none of us to perish and go to hell. And, no I am not condoning repetitive ungodly behavior. I am only saying that it is at God's discretion how we resolve the end of our days. God's Word gave me the peace and confirmation that I was seeking. I am hopeful that the following affirmations will help you along the way. I pray that you seek and then take the right road. But if you find yourself off course, know that the way back is possible. I've seen him do it.

In memory of my sister
Olivia Stewart
February 7, 1964–December 12, 2007

On Attitude

1. The Melding - Your task is not to seek for love, but merely to seek and find all the barriers within yourself that you have built against it.
2. Live your Dreams - You are never given a dream without also being given the power to make it true.
3. If you seek what is honorable, what is good, what is the truth of your life, all the other things you could not imagine come as a matter of course.
4. Dreams are renewable, no matter what our age or condition there are still untapped possibilities within us and new beauty waiting to be born.
5. Truly free, Hold fast to dreams for if dreams die life is a broken-winged bird that cannot fly.
6. You can do it - Just don't give up trying to do what you really want to do. Where there's love and inspiration.
7. I don't think you can go wrong. You are never to old to set another goal or to dream a new dream.
8. Everyone should carefully observe which way his heart draws him and then choose that way with all his strength.
9. On Marriage - How do I love thee? Let me count the ways. I love thee to the depth and breadth and height my soul can reach.
10. The Real thing - If I know what love is, it is because of you. In every union there is a mystery.
11. Love doesn't just sit there like a stone, it has to be made, like bread. Remade all the time, make new. True.
12. Intimacy - love cures people - both the ones who give it and the ones who receive it.
13. On motherhood - God sent children for another purpose than merely to keep up the race to enlarge our hearts and to make us unselfish and full of

13 cont. Kindly sympathies and affections to give our souls higher aims to call out all our faculties to extended enterprise and exertion and to sing round our firesides bright faces, happy smiles and loving, tender hearts. [14] I long to accomplish a great and noble task but it is my chief duty to accomplish small tasks as if they were great and noble.

15 There are high spots in all of our lives and most of them have come about through encouragement from someone else. I don't care how great how famous or successful a man or woman may be, each hungers for applause. [16] Overcome obstacles - walk on a rainbow trail, walk on a trail of song and all about you will be beauty. There is a way out of every dark mist over a rainbow trail. [17] Patience and perseverance have a magical effect before which difficulties disappear obstacles vanish. [18] They can conquer who believe they can. [19] It was a high counsel that I once heard given to a young person, Always do what you are afraid to do. [20] Don't just count your years, make your years count. [21] Special moments - When your life is filled with the desire to see the holiness in everyday life something magical happens

Ordinary life becomes extraordinary. And the very process of life begins to nourish your soul. [22] The cream of enjoyment in this life is always impromptu. The chance walk, the unexpected visit, the unpremeditated journey; the unsought conversation or acquaintance. [23] The stir of delight comes in small ways. [24] That man is richest whose pleasures are cheapest. Miracles [25] Where there is great love there are always miracles. [26] A miracle cannot prove what is impossible; it is useful only to confirm what is possible. [27] A coincidence is a small miracle where God chose to remain anonymous. [28] Across the generations - life is no brief candle to me. It is a sort of splendid torch which I have got hold of for the moment. And I want to make it burn as brightly as possible before handing it on to future generations. [29] Love is patient, love is kind. It does not envy, It does not boast, It is not proud. It is not rude. It is not self-seeking. It is not easily angered, it keeps no record of wrongs. [30] Come death, if you will; you cannot divide us; you can only unite us. [31] Those who love deeply never grow old; they may die of old age, but they die young. [32] Love is something that you can leave behind when you die. It's that powerful.

1. Rumi
2. Richard Bach
3. Oprah Winfrey
4. Dale E. Turner
5. Langston Hughes
6. Ella Fitzgerald
7. C. S. Lewis
8. Hasidic saying
9. Elizabeth Barrett Browning, Sonnet 43
10. Herman Hesse
11. Ursula Le Guin
12. Karl Menninger
13. Mary Botham Howitt
14. Helen Keller
15. George Matthew Adams
16. Robert Motherwell
17. John Quincy Adams
18. Virgil
19. Ralph Waldo Emerson
20. George Meredith
21. Harold S. Kushner
22. Fanny Fern
23. Robert Louis Stevenson
24. Henry David Thoreau
25. Willa Cather
26. Maimonides
27. Author unknown
28. George Bernard Shaw
29. 1 Corinthians 3:14
30. From final letter to a father—Franz Grillparzer
31. Dorothy Canfield Fisher, Ben Franklin, Abigail Van Buren
32. John Fire Lame Deer

SCAN CODE BELOW
Scan the QR Code below to watch a THANK YOU video message from author, Cynthia Hogue.